SCIPIO AFRICANUS

PUBLIUS CORNELIUS SCIPIO AFRICANUS

SCIPIO AFRICANUS
Greater Than Napoleon

B.H. LIDDELL HART

DA CAPO PRESS
A Member of the Perseus Books Group

TO

THE MASTER, FELLOW AND SCHOLARS

OF

CORPUS CHRISTI COLLEGE

CAMBRIDGE

Cataloging-in-Publication data for this book is available from the Library of Congress.

ISBN-10: 0-306-81363-7   ISBN-13: 978-0-306-81363-4

This Da Capo Press paperback edition of *Scipio Africanus* is an unabridged republication of the edition first published as *A Greater Than Napolean: Scipio Africanus* in London in 1926.

Published by Da Capo Press
A Member of the Perseus Books Group
http://www.dacapopress.com

Da Capo Press books are available at special discounts for bulk purchases in the U.S. by corporations, institutions, and other organizations. For more information, please contact the Special Markets Department at the Perseus Books Group, 11 Cambridge Center, Cambridge, MA 02142, or call (800) 255-1514 or (617) 252-5298, or e-mail special.markets@perseusbooks.com.

PREFACE.

THE excuse for this book is that no recent biography of Scipio exists ; the first and last in English appeared in 1817, and is the work of a country clergyman, who omits any study of Scipio as a soldier ! The reason for this book is that, apart from the romance of Scipio's personality and his political importance as the founder of Rome's world-dominion, his military work has a greater value to modern students of war than that of any other great captain of the past. A bold claim, and yet its truth will, I hope, be substantiated in the following pages.

For the study of tactical methods the campaigns of Napoleon or of 1870, even of 1914-1918 perhaps, are as dead as those of the third century B.C. But the art of generalship does not age, and it is because Scipio's battles are richer in stratagems and ruses—many still feasible to-day—than those of any other commander in history that they are an unfailing object-lesson to soldiers.

Strategically Scipio is still more " modern."
The present is a time of disillusionment, when
we are realising that slaughter is not synonymous
with victory, that the " destruction of the
enemy's main armed forces on the battlefield "
is at best but a means to the end, and not an
end in itself, as the purblind apostles of Clausewitz had deceived themselves—and the world,
unhappily.   In the future, even more than in
the past, the need is to study and understand
the interplay of the military, economic, and
political forces, which are inseparable in strategy.
Because Scipio more than any other great captain understood and combined these forces in
his strategy, despite the very " modern " handicap of being the servant of a republic—not, like
Alexander, Frederick, Napoleon, a despot,—the
study of his life is peculiarly apposite to-day.
Above all, because the moral objective was the
aim of all his plans, whether political, strategical,
or tactical.

My grateful thanks are due to Sir Geoffrey
Butler, K.B.E., M.P., Fellow of Corpus Christi
College, Cambridge; to Mr W. E. Heitland, M.A.,
Fellow of St John's College, Cambridge; and to
Mr E. G. Hawke, M.A., Lecturer at Queen's
College, London, for their kindness in reading
the proofs and for helpful comments.

B. H. L. H.

CONTENTS

LIST OF MAPS

INTRODUCTION

THE road to failure is the road to fame—such apparently must be the verdict on posterity's estimate of the world's greatest figures. The flash of the meteor impresses the human imagination more than the remoter splendour of the star, fixed immutably in the high heavens. Is it that final swoop earthwards, the unearthly radiance ending in the common dust, that, by its evidence of the tangible or the finite, gives to the meteor a more human appeal ? So with the luminaries of the human system, provided that the ultimate fall has a dramatic note, the memory of spectacular failure eclipses that of enduring success. Again, it may be that the completeness of his course lends individual emphasis to the great failure, throwing his work into clearer relief, whereas the man whose efforts are crowned with permanent success builds a stepping-stone by which others may advance still farther, and so merges his own fame in that of his successors.

The theory at least finds ample confirmation in the realm of action. A Napoleon and a Lee are enshrined in drama, in novel, and in memoir by the hundred. A Wellington and a Grant are almost forgotten by the writers of the nations they brought through peril intact and victorious. Even a Lincoln may only have been saved from comparative oblivion by the bullet of an assassin, a Nelson by death in the hour of victory, which relieved by emotion-awakening tragedy the disrepute of a successful end. It would seem likely that a century hence the name of Ludendorff will be emblazoned as the heroic figure of the European War, while that of Foch sinks into obscurity ; there are signs already of this tendency to exalt the defeated.

For permanence of reputation a man of action must appeal to emotion, not merely to the mind ; and since the living man himself no longer can kindle the emotions of posterity, the dramatic human touch of ultimate failure is essential. This truth would seem to hold in most branches of human effort. Scott's gallant but unavailing attempt to reach the South Pole lives in the world's memory, while the successful ventures

of Amundsen and Peary are fading. In sport,
Dorando's Marathon is an enduring memory;
but who among the general public could recall
the name of Hayes, the actual victor, or, indeed,
that of any subsequent Marathon winner.

For this irrational, this sentimental verdict,
it is fashionable to fix the blame on modern
journalism, yet the barest survey of history
shows that its origins lie far back in the mists
of time. On the historian, in fact—who of all
men should by training and outlook put his
trust in reason—falls the major responsibility
for this eternal tendency—the glorification of
dramatic failure at the expense of enduring
achievement. The history of the ancient con-
firms that of the modern world, and in no example more strikingly than that of Scipio
Africanus, the subject of this brief study, which
is an attempt to redress the " historical " balance
by throwing further weights of knowledge and
military appreciation on Scipio's side, not as
commonly by detraction from his rivals.
Gradually, progressively, the belittlement of
Scipio has been pressed by historians anxious
to enhance the fame of Hannibal. It is the more
unreasonable, the less excusable, because here
there are no mass of conflicting sources and
contemporary opinions. The reliable data on
which to base a study and a judgment are

practically limited to the works of Polybius
and Livy, with but a few grains from other,
and admittedly less trustworthy, ancient authorities. And of these two, Polybius, the earlier,
is almost contemporary with events, the friend
of Gaius Lælius, Scipio's constant subordinate,
from whom he could get first-hand evidence and
judgments. He had the family archives of the
Scipios at his disposal for research, and he had
been over the actual battlefields while many
of the combatants were still alive. Thus he
gained an almost unique base upon which to
form his estimate.

Further, being a Greek, his views are less
suspect than those of Livy of being coloured
by Roman patriotic bias, while modern historical
criticism is unanimous in its tribute alike to his
impartiality, his thoroughness of research, and
the soundness of his critical insight.

The verdict of Polybius is clear, and his facts
still more so.

That there were divergent judgments of Scipio
among the Romans of succeeding generations is
true ; but Polybius explains the reasons so con-
vincingly, their truth borne out by the known
facts of Scipio's strategical and tactical plans,
that there is no vestige of excuse for modern
writers to regard as due to luck what superstition led the ancients to ascribe to divine aid.

" The fact that he was almost the most famous man of all time makes every one desirous to know what sort of man he was, and what were the natural gifts and the training which enabled him to accomplish so many great actions. But none can help falling into error and acquiring a mistaken impression of him, as the estimate of those who have given us their views about him is very wide of the truth." " . . . They represent him as a man favoured by fortune . . . such men being, in their opinion, more divine and more worthy of admiration than those who always act by calculation. They are not aware that the one deserves praise and the other only congratulation, being common to ordinary men, whereas what is praiseworthy belongs only to men of sound judgment and mental ability, whom we should consider to be the most divine and most beloved by the gods. To me it seems that the character and principles of Scipio much resembled those of Lycurgus, the Lacedæmonian legislator. For neither must we suppose that Lycurgus drew up the constitution of Sparta under the influence of superstition and solely prompted by the Pythia, nor that Scipio won such an empire for his country by following the suggestion of dreams and omens. But since both of them saw that most men neither readily accept any-

thing unfamiliar to them, nor venture on great
risks without the hope of divine help, Lycurgus
made his own scheme more acceptable and more
easily believed in by invoking the oracles of the
Pythia in support of projects due to himself,
while Scipio similarly made the men under his
command more sanguine and more ready to face
perilous enterprises by instilling into them the
belief that his projects were divinely inspired.
But that he invariably acted on calculation and
foresight, and that the successful issue of his
plans was always in accord with rational ex-
pectation, will be evident."

To the mind of to-day not only does such an
explanation appear inherently probable, but
affords a key to the understanding of a man
whose triumphs, whether military, political, or
diplomatic, were, above all, due to his supreme
insight into the psychology of men. Who,
moreover, applied this gift like the conductor
of a great orchestra to the production of a world
harmony. In conducting policy, through war
to peace, he indeed attained a concord which
aptly fulfilled the musical definition : "A combination which both by its . . . smoothness and
by its logical origin and purpose in the scheme
can form a point of repose." As a conductor of
the human orchestra he had, however, two
weaknesses, one inborn and one developing with

years. He could not comprehend the low notes
—the narrowness and baseness to which men
can descend,—and the exaltation of spirit born
of his power over men prevented him from
hearing the first warnings of that discord which
was to impair the glorious symphony so nearly
completed.

SCIPIO

CHAPTER I.

HALF LIGHT.

PUBLIUS CORNELIUS SCIPIO was born at Rome
in the 517th year from the city's foundation—
235 B.C. Though a member of one of the most
illustrious and ancient families, the Cornelii, of
his early years and education no record, not
even an anecdote, has come down to us. Indeed, not until he is chosen, through a combination of circumstances and his own initiative,
to command the army in Spain at the age of
twenty-four, does history give us more than an
occasional fleeting glimpse of his progress. Yet
bare and brief as these are, each is significant.
The first is at the battle of the Ticinus, Hannibal's initial encounter with the Roman arms
on Italian soil, after his famous passage of the
Alps. Here the youthful Scipio, a lad of seventeen, accompanied his father, the Roman commander. If his first experience of battle was
on the losing side, he at least emerged with
enviable distinction. Let the story be told in

Polybius's words : " His father had placed him in command of a picked troop of horse " (in reserve on a small hill) " in order to ensure his safety ; but when he caught sight of his father in the battle, surrounded by the enemy and escorted only by two or three horsemen and dangerously wounded, he at first endeavoured to urge those with him to go to the rescue, but when they hung back for a time owing to the large numbers of the enemy round them, he is said with reckless daring to have charged the encircling force alone. Upon the rest being now forced to attack, the enemy were terror-struck and broke up, and Publius Scipio, thus un-expectedly rescued, was the first to salute his son as his deliverer." It is said that the consul ordered a civic crown, the Roman V.C., to be presented to his son, who refused it, saying that " the action was one that rewarded itself." The exploit does credit to the young Scipio's gallantry, but the outcome, as emphasised by Polybius, does still more credit to his psychological insight. " Having by this service won a universally acknowledged reputation for bravery, he in subsequent times refrained from exposing his person without sufficient reason when his country reposed her hopes of success on him—conduct characteristic not of a commander who relies on luck, but on one gifted with intelligence."

To the present generation, with personal experience of war, the point may have greater force than to the closeted historians. To the former, the higher commander who aspires to be a platoon leader, thrusting himself into the fight at the expense of his proper duty of direction, is not the heroic or inspired figure that he appears to the civilian. To some too, not natural lovers of danger for its own sake—and these are rare in any army,—the point will touch a chord of memory, reminding them of how by the moral hold on their men given by one such exploit they were thereafter enabled to take the personal precautions which better befit the officer entrusted with the lives of others. The civilian at home poured scorn on the German officer "leading" his men from behind; not so the fighting soldier, for he knew that when the occasion called, his officer enemy did not hesitate to risk, nay throw away his life, as an example. The story still lives of the German officer who led a forlorn hope mounted on a white horse.

The exploit, and the popular fame it brought, launched Scipio's military career so auspiciously as to earn him rapid advancement. For, less than two years later, 216 B.C., Livy's account speaks of him as one of the military tribunes, from whom the commanders of the legions were nominated, and in itself a post that made him one of the deputies or staff officers of the legion commander. If a parallel is desired, the nearest modern equivalent is a staff colonel.

This second glimpse of Scipio comes on the morrow of Cannæ, Rome's darkest hour, and it is curious that the future general, who, like Marlborough, was never to fight a battle that he did not win, should in his subordinate days have been witness of unrelieved disaster. There is no record of Scipio's share in the battle, but from Livy's account it seems clear that he was among the ten thousand survivors who escaped to the greater Roman camp across the River Aufidus, and further, one of the undaunted four thousand who, rather than surrender with their fellows, quitted the camp after nightfall, and eluding the Carthaginian horse, made their way to Canusium. Their situation was still perilous, for this place lay only some four miles distant, and why Hannibal did not follow up his success by the destruction of this remnant, isolated from succour, remains one of the enigmas of history, to all appearance a blemish on his generalship.

With the four thousand at Canusium were four military tribunes, and, as Livy tells us, " by the consent of all, the supreme command was vested in Publius Scipio, then a very young man, and Appius Claudius." Once more Scipio shines amid the darkness of defeat; once more a time of general disaster is the opportunity of youth backed by character. Disruption, if not mutiny, threatens. Word is brought that men are saying that Rome is doomed, and that certain of the younger patricians, headed by Lucius Cæcilius Metellus, are proposing to leave Rome to its fate and escape overseas to seek service with some foreign king. These fresh tidings of ill-fortune dismay and almost paralyse the assembled leaders. But while the others urge that a council be called to deliberate upon the situation, Scipio acts. He declares " that it is not a proper subject for deliberation; that courage and action, and not deliberation, were necessary in such a calamity. That those who desired the safety of the state would attend him in arms forthwith; that in no place was the camp of the enemy more truly than where such designs were meditated." Then, with only a few companions, he goes straight to the lodging of Metellus, surprising the plotters in council. Drawing his sword, Scipio proclaims his purpose: " I swear that I will neither desert the cause of Rome, nor allow any other citizen of Rome to desert it. If knowingly I violate this oath, may Jupiter visit with the most horrible perdition my house, my family, and my fortune. I insist that you, Lucius Cæcilius, and

the rest of you present, take this oath; and
let the man who demurs be assured that this
sword is drawn against him." The upshot is
that, " terrified, as though they were beholding
the victorious Hannibal, they all take the oath,
and surrender themselves to Scipio to be kept
in custody."

This danger quelled, Scipio and Appius, hearing that Varro, the surviving consul, had reached
Venusia, sent a messenger there, placing themselves under his orders.

Scipio's next brief entry on the stage of history
is in a different scene. His elder brother, Lucius,
was a candidate for the ædileship,[1] and the
younger Publius " for long did not venture to
stand for the same office as his brother. But
on the approach of the election, judging from the
disposition of the people that his brother had
a poor chance of being elected, and seeing that
he himself was exceedingly popular, he came to
the conclusion that the only means by which
his brother would attain his object would be
by their coming to an agreement and both of
them making the attempt, and so he hit on the

---

[1] The ædileship was normally the first rung of the ladder to
the higher magistracy. Its functions were those of a civic
"Home Office"—the care of the city and the enforcement of
the by-laws, the supervision of the markets and of prices and
measures, the superintendence and organisation of the public
games.

following plan. Seeing that his mother was visiting the different temples and sacrificing to the gods on behalf of his brother and generally showing great concern about the result, he told her, as a fact, that he had twice had the same dream. He had dreamt that both he and his brother had been elected to the ædileship, and were going up from the Forum to their house when she met them at the door and fell on their necks and kissed them. She was affected by this, as a woman would be, and exclaimed, 'Would I might see that day,' or something similar. 'Then would you like us to try, mother?' he said. Upon her consenting, as she never dreamt he would venture on it, but thought it was merely a casual joke—for he was exceedingly young,—he begged her to get a white toga ready for him at once, this being the dress that candidates are in the habit of wearing. What she had said had entirely gone out of her head, and Scipio, waiting until he received the white toga, appeared in the Forum while his mother was still asleep. The people, owing to the unexpectedness of the sight, and owing to his previous popularity, received him with enthusiastic surprise; and afterwards, when he went on to the station appointed for candidates and stood by his brother, they not only conferred the office on Publius but on his brother

too for his sake, and both appeared at their
home elected ædiles. When the news suddenly
reached his mother's ears, she, overjoyed, met
them at the door and embraced the young men
with deep emotion, so that from this circumstance all who had heard of the dreams believed
that Publius communed with the gods not only
in his sleep, but still more in reality and by
day."

"Now, it was not a matter of a dream at all ;
but as he was kind, munificent, and agreeable
in his address, he reckoned on his popularity
with the people, and so by cleverly adapting his
action to the actual sentiment of the people
and of his mother, he not only attained his
object, but was believed to have acted under
a sort of divine inspiration. For those who are
incapable of taking an accurate view of oppor-
tunities, causes, and dispositions, attribute to
the gods and to fortune the causes of what is
accomplished by shrewdness and with calculation and foresight."

To some the deception, even though for a
worthy end, may seem out of tune with the
higher Roman virtues ; and Livy, to whom as
a Roman the artifice would appear less admirable than to Polybius, a Greek, leaves in doubt
the origin of this habit of Scipio's, developed
in his after career either by reason of its success

or practice. Here is Livy's appreciation:
" Scipio was undoubtedly the possessor of striking gifts ; but besides that he had from child-
hood studied the art of their effective display.
Whether there was some vein of superstition in
his own temperament, or whether it was with
the aim of securing for his commands the
authority of inspired utterances, he rarely spoke
in public without pretending to some nocturnal
vision or supernatural suggestion." Livy may
exaggerate the frequency, for he wrote at a
later date, and legends grow round the characteristics of the great. Such supernatural claims
only appear occasionally in Scipio's recorded
utterances, and he, a supreme artist in handling
human nature, would realise the value of re-
serving them for critical moments.

Livy continues : " In order to impress public
opinion in this direction, he had made a practice
from the day he reached manhood of never
engaging in any business, public or private,
without first paying a visit to the Capitol.
There he would enter the sanctuary and pass
some time, generally in solitude and seclusion.
This habit . . . made converts to a belief, to
which accident or design had given wide cur-
rency, that his origin was other than human.
There was a story once widely believed about
Alexander the Great, that his male parent had

been a huge serpent, often seen in his mother's chamber, but vanishing directly men appeared. This miracle was told again of Scipio . . . but he himself never cast ridicule upon it; indeed, he rather lent it countenance by the course which he adopted of neither wholly disclaiming such tales nor openly asserting their truth." This last tale, incidentally, is repeated by several of the ancient writers and enshrined in ' Paradise Lost,' where Milton writes :—

> " He with Olympias, this with her that bore
> Scipio, the height of Rome."

The view that this claim to divine inspiration had a religious and not merely an intellectual basis gains some support from Scipio's conduct in the Syrian War of 190 B.C., when, because he was a member of the college of the priests of Mars, known as Salian priests, he stayed behind the army and indirectly kept it waiting at the Hellespont, as the rule bound him to stay where he was until the month ended.

Again, modern psychologists may suggest that his dreams were true and not invented, such is known to be the power of strong desire to fulfil itself in dreams. Whatever the explanation and the source of his " visions," there can be no doubt as to the skill with which he turned them to practical account. And it is a supreme moral

tribute to Scipio that this power was exerted
by him purely to further his country's good,
never his own. When trouble and accusation
came in later days, and an ungrateful State
forgot its saviour, Scipio did not invoke any
divine vision in his defence. That he so refrained is the more definite and the more significant, because, with other psychological means,
he showed himself still the supreme "organist"
of the human instrument.

Scipio's election to the ædileship is historically
important, not only because it illumines the
sources of his success and influence over men,
but also for its light on the causes of his political
decline, the self-imposed exile from an ungrateful
country, which saw a marvellously brilliant
career close in shadow. It is Livy who shows
that his election was not so unopposed as Polybius's account would suggest ; that the tribunes
of the people opposed his pretensions to the
office because he had not attained the legal
age for candidature. Whereupon Scipio retorted
that " if the citizens in general are desirous of
appointing me ædile, I am old enough "—an
appeal over the heads of the tribunes which was
instantly successful, but which by its triumphant
defiance of tradition and rule was likely to add
resentment to the jealousy which inevitably
accompanies the precocious success of youth.

CHAPTER II.

DAWN.

THESE three episodes form the prologue to the
real drama of Scipio's career. On this the curtain rises in 210 B.C., which, if not Rome's
blackest hour in her life and death struggle
with Carthage, was at least the greyest. That
conflict, which she had entered upon originally
in 264 B.C., was the inevitable sequel to the
supremacy of the Italian peninsula won by
her combination of political genius and military
vigour, for this supremacy could never be secure
so long as an alien sea power—Carthage—commanded the waters of the peninsula, a continual
menace to its seaboard and commerce. But
when, after many hazards, the close of the First
Punic War in 241 B.C. yielded Rome this mari-
time security, the vision and ambition of Hamilcar Barca not merely revived, but widened the
scope of the struggle between Rome and Carthage into one with world power or downfall

as the stakes. During the long interval of outward peace this Carthaginian Bismarck prepared the mental and material means for a stroke at the heart of the Roman power, educating his sons and followers to conceive the conquest of Rome as their goal, and using Spain as the training ground for the Barcine school of war, as well as the base of their forthcoming military effort. In 218 B.C., Hannibal, crossing the Alps, began his invasion of Italy to reap the harvest for which his father had sown the seeds. His victories on the Ticinus, the Trebia, at the Trasimene Lake, grew in scale until they reached their apex on the battlefield of Cannæ. If Roman fortitude, the loyalty of most of the Italian allies, and Hannibal's strategic caution then gained for Rome a reprieve, the passage of five years' unceasing warfare so drained her resources and exhausted her allies that by 211 B.C. Roman power, internally if not superficially, was perhaps nearer than ever before to a breakdown. A machine that is new and in good condition can withstand repeated severe shocks, but when badly worn a jar may suffice to cause its collapse. Such a jar came, for while Hannibal was campaigning in Southern Italy, destroying Roman armies if apparently drawing no nearer his object—the destruction of the Roman power,— the Carthaginian arms in Spain had been crowned with a victory that threatened Rome's footing on the peninsula.

For several years Scipio's father and uncle, Publius the elder and Gnæus, had been in command of the Roman forces there, winning repeated successes until, caught divided, the two brothers were defeated in turn, both falling on the battlefield. The shattered remnants of the Roman forces were driven north of the Ebro, and only a gallant rally by Marcius prevented the Romans being driven out of Spain. Even so their situation was precarious, for many of the Spanish tribes had forsaken the Romans in their hour of adversity. Though the determination of Rome itself, as before, was unbroken, and the disaster only spurred her to retrieve it, the choice of a successor proved difficult. Finally, it was decided to call an assembly of the people to elect a pro-consul for Spain. But no candidates offered themselves for the dangerous honour. " The people, at their wits' end, came down to the Campus Martius on the day of the election, where, turning towards the magistrate, they looked round at the countenances of their most eminent men, who were earnestly gazing at each other, and murmured bitterly that their affairs were in so ruinous a state, and the condition of the commonwealth so desperate, that no one dared under-

take the command in Spain. When suddenly
Publius Cornelius, son of Publius who had fallen
in Spain, who was about twenty-four years of
age, declared himself a candidate, and took his
station on an eminence by which he could be
seen by all " (Livy). His election was unanimous,
not only by every century, but by every man
there present. " But after the business had
been concluded, and the ardour and impetuosity
of their zeal had subsided, a sudden silence
ensued, and a secret reflection on what they
had done—whether their partiality had not got
the better of their judgment. They chiefly
regretted his youth ; but some were terrified
at the fortune which attended his house and
his name, for while the two families to which
he belonged were in mourning, he was going into
a province where he must carry on his operations amid the tombs of his father and his
uncle."

Realising the prevalence of these second
thoughts, these doubts, Scipio sought to offset
them by summoning an assembly, at which his
sagacious arguments did much to restore confidence. The secret of his sway, extraordinary
in one so young, over the crowd mind, especially
in times of crisis, was his profound self-confidence, which radiated an influence to which
the stories of his divine inspiration were but

auxiliary. Self-confidence is a term often used
in a derogatory sense, but Scipio's was not only
justified by results but essentially different, a
spiritual exaltation which is epitomised by Aulus
Gellius as " conscientia sui subnixus "—" lifted
high on his consciousness of himself."

To the remains of the army in Spain ten
thousand foot and a thousand horse were added,
and taking these reinforcements, Scipio set sail
with a fleet of thirty quinqueremes from the
mouth of the Tiber. Coasting along the Gulf
of Genoa, the Riviera shore, and the Gulf of
Lions, he landed his troops just inside the
Spanish frontier, and then marched overland
to Tarraco—modern Tarragona. Here he received embassies from the various Spanish
allies. His appreciation of the moral factor
and of the value of personal observation, two
vital elements in generalship, was shown in his
earliest steps. The rival forces were in winter
quarters, and before attempting to formulate
any plan he visited the States of his allies and
every one of the various parts of his army,
seeking always by his attitude, even more than
by his words, to rekindle confidence and dissi-
pate the influence of past defeat. His own
moral stature could not be better shown than by
his treatment of Marcius, the man who had
partly retrieved the Roman disasters, and thus

one whom an ambitious general might well regard as a rival to his own position and fame. But "Marcius he kept with him, and treated him with such respect that it was perfectly clear that there was nothing he feared less than lest any one should stand in the way of his own glory." Napoleon's jealousy of Moreau, his deliberate overshadowing of his own marshals, is in marked contrast with Scipio's attitude, and one of the finest of military tributes to him is the abiding affection felt for him by his subordinate generals. "No man is a hero to his valet," and but few generals are heroes to their chief staff officers, who see them intimately in their nude qualities beneath the trappings of authority and public reputation. Loyal subordinates will maintain the fiction of infallibility for the good of the army, and so long as is necessary, but they know the man as he is, and in later years the truth leaks out. Thus it is worth remembering that the verdict of Polybius is founded on direct conversations with Gaius Lælius, Scipio's coadjutor, and the one man to whom he confided his military plans before operations.

To the soldiers suffering under defeat he made no reproaches, but aptly mingled an appeal to their reason and to their spirit, reminding them how often in Roman history early defeat had been the presage to ultimate victory, how the sure tilting of the balance had already begun, the initial disasters found their counterpoise, and in Italy and Sicily everything was going prosperously. Then he pointed out that the Carthaginian victories were not due to superior courage, but " to the treachery of the Celti- berians and to rashness, the generals having been cut off from each other owing to their trust in the alliance of that people." Next he showed how their disadvantages had shifted to the other side, the Carthaginian armies " being en- camped a long distance apart," their allies estranged by tactlessness and tyranny, and, above all, personal ill-feeling between the enemy's commanders would make them slow to come to each other's assistance. Finally, he kindled their enthusiasm by touching their affection for their lost leaders : " I will soon bring it to pass that, as you can now trace in me a likeness to my father and uncle in my features, counte- nance, and figure, I will so restore a copy of their genius, honour, and courage, that every man of you shall say that his commander, Scipio, has either returned to life, or has been born again."

His first step was to restore and fortify the confidence of his own troops and allies, his next to attack that of his enemies, to strike not at

their flesh but at their moral Achilles heel. His
acute strategical insight, in a day when strategy,
as distinct from battle tactics, had hardly been
born, made him realise that Spain was the real
key to the whole struggle. Spain was Hannibal's real base of operations ; there he had
trained his armies, and thence he looked for
his reinforcements.

Scipio's first move was to apply his appreciation of the moral objective within the Spanish
theatre of war.   While others urged him to
attack one of the Carthaginian armies, he decided
to strike at their base, their life-line. First, he
concentrated all his troops at one place, leaving
one small but compact detachment of 3000 foot
and 300 horse under Marcus Silanus to secure
his own essential pivot of operations—Tarraco.
Then, with all the rest, 25,000 foot and 2500 horse
—here was true economy of force,—he crossed
the Ebro, " revealing his plan to no one."
" The fact was that he had decided not to do
any of the things he had publicly announced,
but to invest suddenly " New Carthage—modern
Cartagena. To this end " he gave secret orders
to Gaius Lælius, who commanded the fleet,
who alone was aware of the project, to sail
to that place, while he himself with his
land forces marched rapidly against it."   As
Polybius sagely emphasises, calculation marked

this youth, for " he, in the first place, took in
hand a situation pronounced by most people as
desperate . . . and secondly, in dealing with it
he put aside the measures obvious to any one,
and planned out and decided on a course which
neither his enemies nor his friends expected."
" On his arrival in Spain he . . . inquired from
every one about the circumstances of the enemy,
and learnt that the Carthaginian forces were
divided into three bodies," Mago, near the pillars
of Hercules—Gibraltar ; Hasdrubal, son of Gisco,
near the mouth of the Tagus ; and Hasdrubal
Barca besieging a city in Central Spain not far
from modern Madrid.   None of them were
within less than ten days' march from New
Carthage ; he himself, as the event proved, was
within seven days' forced marches of it.   The
news of his attack must take several days to
reach them, and if he could take it by a surprise
coup de main he would forestall any aid, and
" in the event of failure he could, since he was
master of the sea, place his troops in a position
of safety."   Polybius further tells us how " during the winter he made detailed inquiries from
people acquainted with it."   " He learnt that
it stood almost alone among Spanish cities in
possessing harbours fit for a fleet and for naval
forces, and also that it was for the Carthaginians
the direct sea crossing from Africa.   Next he

heard that the Carthaginians kept the bulk of
their money and their war material in this city,
as well as their hostages from the whole of
Spain ; and, what was of most importance, that
the trained soldiers who garrisoned the citadel
were only about a thousand strong, because no
one dreamt that while the Carthaginians were
masters of nearly the whole of Spain it would
enter any one's head to besiege the city, while
the remaining population was exceedingly large,
but composed of artisans, tradesmen, and sailors,
men very far from having any military experience. This he considered to be a thing that
would tell against the city if he appeared suddenly before it "—the moral calculation again.
"Abandoning, therefore, all other projects, he
spent his time while in winter quarters in preparing for this," but "he concealed the plan
from every one except Gaius Lælius." The
account shows that he was master of two more
attributes of generalship—the power to keep
his intentions secret until their disclosure was
necessary for the execution of the plan, and the
wisdom to realise that military success depends
largely on the thoroughness of the previous
preparation.

Polybius's assertion that Scipio's move was
due to masterly calculation, and not to inspiration or fortune, is confirmed indirectly by the

reference to a letter of Scipio's which he had seen, and directly by Livy's quotation of Scipio's speech to the troops before the attack. One phrase epitomises the strategic idea : " You will in actuality attack the walls of a single city, but in that single city you will have made yourselves masters of all Spain," and he explains exactly how capture of the hostages, the treasure, and the war stores will be turned to their advantage and react to the enemy's disadvantage, moral, economic, and material. Even if Livy's phrase was coined to meet Scipio's fact, its note is so exactly in accord with Scipio's actions as to give it a ring of basic truth.

CHAPTER III.

THE STORM OF CARTAGENA.

ON the seventh day from the start of the march
Scipio arrived before the city and encamped,
the fleet arriving simultaneously in the harbour,
thus cutting off communication on all sides.
This harbour formed a circular bottle, its mouth
almost corked by an island, while Cartagena
itself was like a candle stuck in the bottom of
the bottle, the city standing on a narrow rocky
spit of land protruding from the mainland. This
small peninsula bore a distinct resemblance to
Gibraltar, and the isthmus joining it to the
mainland was only some four hundred yards
across. The city was guarded on two sides by
the sea, and on the west by a lagoon. Here
was a hard nut to crack, seemingly impregnable
to any action save a blockade, and this, time
prevented.

Scipio's first step was to ensure his tactical
security by defending the outer side of his camp
with a palisade and double trench stretching

from sea to sea. On the inner side, facing the
isthmus, he erected no defences, partly because
the nature of the ground gave protection, and
partly in order not to hinder the free movement
of his assaulting troops. The Carthaginian commander, Mago, to oppose him armed two thousand of the sturdiest citizens, and posted them
by the landward gate for a sortie. The rest he
distributed to defend the walls to the best of
their power, while of his own regulars he disposed five hundred in the citadel on the top of .
the peninsula, and five hundred on the eastern
hill.

Next day Scipio encircled the city with ships,
throwing a constant stream of missiles, and about
the third hour [1] sent forward along the isthmus
two thousand picked men with the ladder-bearers,
for its narrowness prevented a stronger force
being deployed. Appreciating the handicap of
their cramped position if counter-attacked by
the yet unshaken defenders, he astutely designed
to turn this handicap to his own advantage.
The expected sortie came as soon as Scipio
sounded the bugle for assault, and a close-
matched struggle ensued. " But as the assistance sent to either side was not equal, the Carthaginians arriving through a single gate and
from a longer distance, the Romans from close

[1] The Roman day began at sunrise.

by and from several points, the battle for this reason was an unequal one. For Scipio had purposely posted his men close to the camp itself in order to entice the enemy as far out as possible " (Livy says the Roman advanced troops retired according to orders on the reserves), "well knowing that if he destroyed those who were, so to speak, the steel edge of the population he would cause universal dejection, and none of those inside would venture out of the gate again " (Polybius). This last point was essential for the freedom of his decisive move.

By the skilful infusion of successive reserves into the combat, the Carthaginian onset was first stemmed and then driven back in disorder, the pursuit being pressed so promptly that the Romans nearly succeeded in forcing an entrance on the heels of the fugitives. Even as it was, the scaling ladders were able to be put up in full security, but the great height of the walls hampered the escaladers, and the assault was beaten off. Polybius gives a picture of the Roman commander during this phase which reveals how he combined personal influence and control with the duty of avoiding rash exposure : " Scipio took part in the battle, but studied his safety as far as possible, for he had with him three men carrying large shields, who, holding these close, covered the surface exposed to the wall, and so afforded him protection." " . . . Thus he could both see what was going on, and being seen by all his men he inspired the combatants with great spirit. The consequence was that nothing was omitted which was necessary in the engagement, but the moment that circumstances suggested any step to him, he set to work at once to do what was necessary."

In modern war no feature has told more heavily against decisive results than the absence of the commander's personal observation and control. Scipio's method, viewed in the light of modern science, may suggest a way to revive this influence. Peradventure the commander of the future will go aloft in an aeroplane, protected by a patrol of fighters, and in communication by wireless telephony with his staff.

Scipio had achieved his first object of wearing down the defenders, and checking the likelihood of further interference with his plans from Carthaginian sorties. The way was thus paved for his next decisive move. To develop this he was only waiting for the ebb of the tide, and this design had been conceived by him long since at Tarraco, where, from inquiries among fishermen who knew Cartagena, he had learnt that at low water the lagoon was fordable.

For this project he assembled five hundred

men with ladders on the shore of the lagoon,
and meanwhile reinforced his forces in the isthmus
with both men and ladders, enough to ensure
that in the next direct assault " the whole extent
of the walls should be covered with escaladers "
—an early example of the modern tactical axiom
that a " fixing " attack should be on the broadest
possible front in order to occupy the enemy's
attention and prevent him turning to meet
the decisive blow elsewhere.   He launched this
assault simultaneously with a landing attack by
the fleet, and when it was at its height " the
tide began to ebb and the water gradually re-
ceded from the edge of the lagoon, a strong and
deep current setting in through the channel to
the neighbourhood, so that to those who were
not prepared for the sight the thing appeared
incredible.   But Scipio had his guides ready,
and bade all the men told off for this service
enter the water and have no fear.   He, indeed,
possessed a particular talent for inspiring confidence and sympathy in his troops when he
called upon them.   Now when they obeyed and
raced through the shallow water, it struck the
whole army that it was the work of some god
. . . and their courage was redoubled " (Polybius).   Of this episode Livy says : " Scipio,
crediting this discovery, due to his own diligence
and penetration, to the gods and to miracle,

which had turned the course of the sea, withdrawn it from the lake, and opened ways never
before trodden by human feet to afford a passage
to the Romans, ordered them to follow Neptune
as their guide." But it is interesting to see that,
while exploiting the moral effect of this idea,
he made practical use of less divine guides. The
five hundred passed without difficulty through
the lagoon, reached the wall, and mounted it
without opposition, because all the defenders
" were engaged in bringing succour to that
quarter in which the danger appeared." " The
Romans having once taken the wall, at first
marched along it, sweeping the enemy off it."
They were clearly imbued with the principle
that a penetration must be promptly widened
before it is deepened—a principle which in the
war of 1914-1918 was only learnt after hard
lessons, at Loos and elsewhere. Next they con-
verged on the landward gate, already assailed
in front, and taking the defenders in rear and
by surprise, overpowered the resistance and
opened the way for the main body of the attackers. The walls thus captured, Scipio at once
exploited his success. For while the mass of
those who had by now scaled the walls set about
the customary massacre of the townsmen, Scipio
himself took care to keep in regular formation
those who entered by the gate, and led them

against the citadel. Here Mago, once he " saw that the city had undoubtedly been captured," surrendered.

If the massacre of the townspeople is revolting to modern ideas, it was the normal custom then and for many centuries thereafter, and with the Romans was a deliberate policy aimed at the moral factor rather than mere insensate slaughter. The direct blow at the civil population, who are the seat of the hostile will, may indeed be revived by the potentialities of aircraft, which can jump, halmawise, over the armed " men " who form the shield of the enemy nation. Such a course, if militarily practicable, is the logical one, and ruthless logic usually overcomes the humaner sentiments in a life and death struggle.

Proof of the discipline of Scipio's troops is that the massacre ceased on a signal after the citadel surrendered, and only then did the troops begin pillaging. The massacre, however difficult for modern minds to excuse, was a military measure, and the conduct of the action was not impeded by the individual's desire to obtain loot or " souvenirs "—an undisciplined impulse which has affected even recent battles.

The massacre, moreover, was partly offset by Scipio's generous, if diplomatic, conduct to the vanquished, once the initial ruthlessness had

achieved its purpose of quenching the citizens'
will to resist. Of the ten thousand male prisoners,
he set free all who were citizens of New Carthage,
and restored their property. The artisans, to
the number of two thousand, he declared the
property of Rome, but promised them their
freedom when the war was over if they " showed
goodwill and industry in their several crafts."
The pick of the remainder were taken for sea
service, thus enabling him to man the captured
vessels and so increase the size of his fleet ; these
also were promised their freedom after the final
defeat of Carthage.   Even to Mago and the
other Carthaginian leaders he acted as became
a chivalrous victor, ordering Lælius to pay them
due attention, until subsequently they were sent
to Rome in the latter's charge, as a tangible
evidence of victory which would revive the
Romans' spirits, and lead them to redouble their
efforts to support him.   Finally, he won new
allies for himself by his kindness to the Spanish
hostages, for instead of retaining them in his
custody as unwilling guarantees, he sent them
home to their own States.

Two incidents, related by both Livy and
Polybius, throw Scipio's character into relief,
and enhance his reputation as one of the most
humane and far-sighted of the great conquerors.
" When one of the captive women, the wife of

Mandonius, who was brother to Andobales, King
of the Ilergetes, fell at his feet and entreated
him with tears to treat them with more proper
consideration than the Carthaginians had done,
he was touched, and asked her what they stood
in need of. . . . Upon her making no reply, he
sent for the officials appointed to attend on the
women. When they presented themselves, and
assured him that they kept the women generously supplied with all they required, she repeated her entreaty, upon which Scipio was
still more puzzled, and conceiving the idea that
the officials were neglecting their duty and had
now made a false statement, he bade the woman
be of good cheer, saying that he would himself
appoint other attendants, who would see to it
that they were in want of nothing. The old
lady, after some hesitation, said, ' General, you
do not take me rightly if you think that our
present petition is about our food.' Scipio
then understood what she meant, and noticing
the youth and beauty of the daughters of Andobales and the other princes, he was forced to
tears, recognising in how few words she had
pointed out to him the danger to which they
were exposed. So now he made it clear to her
that he understood, and grasping her hand bade
her and the rest be of good cheer, for he would
look after them as if they were his own sisters

and children, and would appoint trustworthy men to attend on them " (Polybius).

The second incident, as told by Polybius, was : " Some young Romans came across a girl of surpassing bloom and beauty, and being aware that Scipio was fond of women brought her to him . . . saying that they wished to make a present of the damsel to him. He was overcome and astonished by her beauty, and he told them that had he been in a private position no present would have been more welcome, but as he was the general it would be the least welcome of any. . . . So he expressed his gratitude to the young men, but called the girl's father, and handing her over to him, at once bade him give her in marriage to whomever of the citizens he preferred. The self-restraint and moderation Scipio showed on this occasion secured him the warm approbation of his troops." Livy's account enlarges the picture, saying that she was previously betrothed to a young chief of the Celtiberians, named Allucius, who was desperately enamoured of her ; that Scipio, hearing this, sent for Allucius and presented her to him ; and that when his parents pressed thank-offerings upon him, he gave these to Allucius as a dowry from himself. This kindly and tactful act not only spread his praises through the Spanish tribes, but earned a more tangible reinforcement, for Allucius reappeared a few days later with fourteen hundred horsemen to join Scipio.

With his own troops also his blend of generosity and wisdom was no less noticeable. The booty was scrupulously divided according to the Roman custom, which ensured that all was pooled; and as he had so cleverly used every art to inspire them beforehand, so now he appreciated the moral value of praise and distinctive reward for feats achieved. Better still was his haste to make the victory secure against any unforeseen slip or enemy counter-stroke. He had led back the legions to their entrenched camp on the same day as the city's capture, leaving Lælius with the marines to guard the city. Then, after one day's rest, he began a course of military exercises to keep the troops up to concert pitch. On the first day the soldiers had to double three and a half miles in their armour, and the legions carried out various drill movements; the second day they had to polish up, repair, and examine their arms; the third day they rested; and the fourth day they carried out weapon training, "some of them swordfighting with wooden swords covered with leather and with a button on the point, while others practised javelin throwing, the javelins also having a button on the point"; on the fifth day they began the course again, and continued during their stay at Cartagena. "The rowers and marines, pushing out to sea when the weather was calm, made trial of the manœuvring of their ships in mock sea-fights." "The general went round to all the works with equal attention. At one time he was employed in the dockyard with his fleet, at another he exercised with the legions; sometimes he would devote himself to the inspection of the works, which every day were carried out with the greatest eagerness by a multitude of artificers, both in the workshops and in the armoury and docks " (Livy).

Then, when the walls had been repaired, he left adequate detachments to hold the city, and set out for Tarraco with the army and the fleet.

In summing up this first brilliant exploit in command, the first tribute is due to the strategic vision and judgment shown in the choice of Cartagena as his objective. Those who exalt the main armed forces of the enemy as the primary objective are apt to lose sight of the fact that the destruction of these is only a means to the end, which is the subjugation of the hostile will. In many cases this means is essential—the only safe one, in fact; but in other cases the opportunity for a direct and secure blow at the enemy's base may offer itself, and of its possibility and value this master-stroke of

Scipio's is an example, which deserves the reflection of modern students of war.

In the sphere of tactics there is a lesson in his consummate blending of the principles of surprise and security, first in the way he secured every offensive move from possible interference or mischance, second in the way he " fixed " the enemy before, and during, his decisive manœuvre.   To strike at an enemy who preserves his freedom of action is to risk hitting the air and being caught off one's balance.   It is to gamble on chances, and the least mischance is liable to upset the whole plan.   Yet how often in war, and even in peace-time manœuvres, have commanders initiated some superficially brilliant manœuvre only to find that the enemy have slipped away from the would-be knockout, because the assailant forgot the need of " fixing."   And the tactical formula of *fixing plus decisive manœuvre* is, after all, but the domestic proverb, " First catch your hare, then cook it."   Precept, however, is simpler than practice, and not least of Scipio's merits is his superb calculation of the time factor in his execution of the formula.

CHAPTER IV.

THE BATTLE OF BÆCULA.

WITH Cartagena in his grip, Scipio had gained
the strategical initiative, which is by no means
identical with the offensive. To attack the
Carthaginian field armies while he was still
markedly inferior in numbers would be to throw
away this advantage and imperil all that he
had gained. On the other hand, he held the
key to any possible Carthaginian move. If
they moved to regain Cartagena, itself impregnable if adequately garrisoned, and still more
so when the defender had command of the sea,
he lay on their flank with his main striking
force. If they moved against him, he would
have the advantage of choosing his own ground,
and, in addition, Cartagena would threaten their
rear, for his command of the sea would enable
him to transfer forces there. If they remained
passive, and this inaction proved their choice,
they would suffer the handicap due to the loss
of their base, depot, and main line of communica-

tion with Carthage. Nothing could have suited
Scipio better, for the respite allowed the moral
effect of Cartagena's capture to sink into the
minds of the Spanish, and allowed him also
time to win over fresh allies to offset his numerical
handicap. The result proved the soundness of
his calculations, for during the next winter
Edeco, Andobales, and Mandonius, three of the
most powerful chieftains in Spain, came over
to him, and most of the Iberian tribes followed
their example. As Polybius justly says, "Those
who have won victories are far more numerous
than those who have used them to advantage,"
and Scipio, more than any other great captain,
seems to have grasped the truth that the fruits
of victory lie in the after years of peace—a truth
hardly realised even to-day, despite the lessons
of Versailles.

The outcome was that Hasdrubal Barca, faced
with this shifting of the balance, felt forced to
take the offensive. This gage Scipio, thus reinforced, was not loth to accept, for it promised
him the chance to deal with one hostile army
before the others had joined it. But with the
principle of security impressed on his mind, he
still further strengthened his forces, to meet the
possibility that he might be forced to fight more
than one army at once. This he did by the
ingenious measure of hauling his ships on shore

at Tarraco and adding their crews to his army,
a course which was feasible because the Carthaginian ships had been swept from the sea,
and because he was about to advance into
the interior.   His foresight in exploiting the
workshop resources of Cartagena gave him an
ample reserve of weapons from which to arm
them.

While Hasdrubal was still preparing, Scipio
moved.   On his advance from his winter quarters
he was joined by Andobales and Mandonius with
their forces, handing over to them their daughters,
whom he had apparently retained—because of
their key importance,—unlike the other hostages
taken at Cartagena.   Next day he made a treaty
with them, of which the essential part was that
they should follow the Roman commanders and
obey their orders.   Scipio evidently appreciated
the importance of unity of command.   The army
of Hasdrubal lay in the district of Castalon, near
the town of Bæcula on the upper reaches of the
Bætis, to-day called the Guadalquiver.   On the
approach of the Romans he shifted his camp
to an admirable defensive position—a small but
high plateau, deep enough for security, and wide
enough to deploy his troops, difficult of access
on the flanks, and with a river protecting its
rear.   The formation of this plateau, moreover,
was in two " steps," and on the lower Hasdrubal

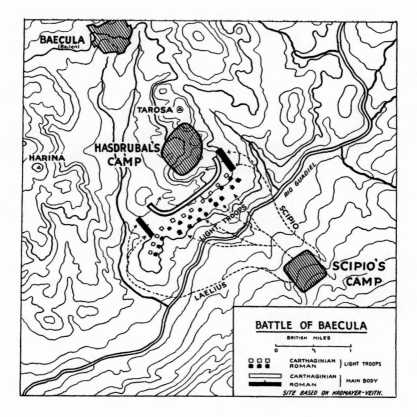

BAECULA
(Bailen)

TAROSA

HASDRUBAL'S
CAMP

HARINA

RIO GUADIEL

SCIPIO

LIGHT TROOPS

LAELIUS

SCIPIO'S
CAMP

BATTLE OF BAECULA

BRITISH MILES

0   ½   1

◻ ◻ ◻   CARTHAGINIAN ⎫
■ ■ ■   ROMAN   ⎭ LIGHT TROOPS

▬▬▬   CARTHAGINIAN ⎫
▬▬▬   ROMAN   ⎭ MAIN BODY

SITE BASED ON KROMAYER-VEITH.

posted his screen of light troops, Numidian horse and Balearic slingers, while on the higher ridge behind he entrenched his camp.

Scipio for a moment was at a loss how to tackle such a strong position, but not daring to wait lest the two other Carthaginian armies should come up, he devised a plan. He sent the velites and other light troops to scale the first " step " of the enemy's position, and despite the rocky ascent and the shower of darts and stones, their determination and practice in using cover enabled them to gain the crest. Once a footing was secured, their better weapons and training for close combat prevailed over skirmishers trained for missile action with ample space for a running fight. Thus the Carthaginian light troops were driven back in disorder on the higher ridge.

Scipio, who had the rest of his army ready but inside their camp, " now despatched the whole of his light troops with orders to support the frontal attack," while, dividing his heavy foot into two bodies, he himself led one half round the left flank of the enemy's position, and sent Lælius with the other to skirt the opposite flank of the ridge until he could find a good line of ascent. Making the shorter circuit, Scipio's men climbed the ridge first, and fell on the Car- thaginians' flank before they had properly deployed, as Hasdrubal, relying on the strength of his position, had delayed leading his main forces out of the camp. Thus trapped before they had formed up and while still on the move, the Carthaginians were thrown into disorder, and during the confusion Lælius came up and charged their other flank. It may be mentioned that Livy, in contradiction to Polybius, says that Scipio led the left wing and Lælius the right, a divergence obviously due to whether the position is considered from the attackers' or the defenders' side.

Polybius states that Hasdrubal's original intention in case of a reverse had been to retreat to Gaul, and after recruiting as many of the natives as possible, to join his brother Hannibal in Italy. Whether this be surmise or fact, as soon as Hasdrubal realised the battle was lost he hurried from the hill with his treasure and his elephants, and collecting in his retreat as many of the fugitives as he could, retired up the river Tagus in the direction of the Pyrenees. But Scipio's double envelopment, and still more his foresight in sending beforehand two cohorts to block two of the main lines of retreat, caught as in a net the bulk of the Carthaginian troops. Eight thousand were slain, twelve thousand taken prisoners. While the African prisoners were sold as slaves, Scipio once more showed his political sagacity by sending home the Spanish prisoners without ransom.

Polybius says, " Scipio did not think it advisable to follow Hasdrubal, as he was afraid of being attacked by the other generals," and to a military critic the reason is convincing. It would have been foolhardy to press farther into the mountainous interior with two more hostile armies, superior in strength, able to converge on him or to cut him off from his base. A bare statement of the military problem is ample answer to those, mainly civil historians, who decry Scipio on the score that he allowed Hasdrubal to quit Spain and move into Italy on his ill-fated attempt to join Hannibal. It is interesting to note that Hasdrubal followed the route of Wellington after Vittoria, making his way to the northern coast of Spain, and crossing by modern San Sebastian and the western gap where the Pyrenees slope down to the sea.

To pretend that Scipio, had he remained on the defensive, could have barred this passage is absurd, based as he was on the eastern coast. Either of the other Carthaginian armies could have contained him while Hasdrubal slipped through one of the numerous western passes, or again, if he attempted so distant a move through wild and mountainous country, not only would he have exposed his base but have

invited disaster. But for Scipio's offensive and
victory at Bæcula, Hasdrubal could have entered
Gaul in force, and thus have avoided the two
years' delay—so fatal to the Carthaginian cause
—enforced by his need to recruit and reorganise
his army in Gaul before passing on.

The aftermath of Bæcula, like that of Cartagena, contains two incidents which illumine
Scipio's character. The first was when the
Spanish allies, old and new, all saluted him as
king. Edeco and Andobales had done so when
joining him on the outward march, and he had
then paid little attention, but when the title
was re-echoed so universally he took action.
Summoning them to an assembly, he " told
them that he wished to be called kingly by
them and actually to be kingly, but that he
did not wish to be king or to be called so by
any one. After saying this he ordered them
to call him general " (Polybius). Livy, relating
this incident in other words, adds, " Even barbarians were sensible of the greatness of mind
which from such an elevation could despise a
name, at the greatness of which the rest of mankind was overawed." It is assuredly the clearest
indication of Scipio's mental stature that in the
first flush of triumph this youthful conqueror
could preserve such self-command and balance
of mind. Weighed solely by his character, apart

from his achievements, Scipio has claims to be
considered the highest embodiment of the Roman
virtues, humanised and broadened by the culture
of Greece, yet proof against its degenerate
tendencies.

The second incident, whether it be due solely
to the sympathetic insight which peculiarly distinguished him or to the diplomatic foresight
which made this gift of such inestimable value
to his country, is equally significant.   The
quæstor selling the African prisoners came upon
a handsome boy, and learning that he was of
royal blood, sent him to Scipio.   In answer to
the latter's questions, the boy said that he was
a Numidian, his name Massiva, and that he had
come to Spain with his uncle Masinissa, who
had raised a force of cavalry to assist the Carthaginians.   That, disobeying his uncle, who considered him too young to be in battle, " he had
clandestinely taken a horse and arms, and,
without his uncle's knowledge, gone on the field,
where, his horse falling, he was thrown and taken
prisoner."   Scipio asked him whether he wished
to return to Masinissa, and on his assenting with
tears of joy, presented the youth with " a gold
ring, a vest with broad purple border, a Spanish
cloak with gold clasp, and a horse completely
caparisoned, and then released him, ordering
a party of horse to escort him as far as he chose."

Scipio then fell back on his base, and spent the remainder of the summer in exploiting the effect of the victory by securing the alliance of most of the Spanish States. His wisdom in not following up Hasdrubal was justified by the fact that within a few days after the battle of Bæcula, Hasdrubal, son of Gisco, and Mago arrived to join Hasdrubal Barca. This arrival, too late to save the last-named from defeat, served to bring about a conference to settle their future plans. Realising that Scipio by his diplomacy and his victories had gained the sympathies of almost all Spain, they decided that Mago should transfer his forces to Hasdrubal Barca, and go to the Balearic Isles to raise fresh auxiliaries; that Hasdrubal Barca should move into Gaul as soon as possible before his remaining Spanish troops deserted, and then march on into Italy; that Hasdrubal, son of Gisco, should retire into the remotest part of Lusitania, near Gades—modern Cadiz,—where alone the Carthaginians might hope for Spanish aid. Finally, Masinissa, with a body of three thousand horse, was to have a roving commission, his object being to harass and ravage the lands of the Romans and of their Spanish allies.

The chronology of these years is somewhat difficult to determine, but the victory at Bæcula

seems to have been in 208 B.C. The next year
Scipio's hold on the country was threatened
afresh. A new general, Hanno, had come with
a fresh army from Carthage to replace Hasdrubal
Barca. Mago also had returned from the Balearic
Isles, and after arming native levies in Celti-
beria, which embraced parts of modern Arragon
and Old Castile, was joined by Hanno. Nor
was the threat only from one direction, for
Hasdrubal, son of Gisco, had advanced from
Gades into Bætica (Andalusia). If Scipio moved
into the interior against Hanno and Mago he
might find Hasdrubal across his rear. Therefore
he detached his lieutenant, Silanus, with ten
thousand foot and five hundred horse, to attack
the former, while he himself apparently kept
watch and check on Hasdrubal.

Silanus marched so fast, despite the rugged
defiles and thick woods on his route, that he
came on the Carthaginians before any messengers
or even rumours had warned them of his approach. The advantage of surprise offset his
inferior strength, and falling first on the Celtiberian camp, where no proper watch or guard
was kept, he had routed them before the Carthaginians had come up to their aid. Mago
with almost all the cavalry and two thousand
foot fled from the field as soon as the verdict

was clear, and retreated towards the province
of Gades.   But Hanno and those of the Carthaginians who arrived on the field when the
battle was decided were taken prisoners, and
the Celtiberian levies so thoroughly dispersed
as to nip in the bud the danger that other
tribes might copy their example and join the
Carthaginians.

It is characteristic of Scipio that he was un-
stinting in his praise of Silanus.   Having thus
ensured the security of his flank for an advance
southward, he moved against Hasdrubal, whereupon the latter not only fell back in indecent
haste, but lest his united army should attract
Scipio on to him, he broke it up to form small
garrisons for the various walled towns.

Scipio, seeing the enemy thus abandon himself to a passive defensive, decided that there
was no object in conducting a series of petty
sieges likely to drain his own force without
adequate advantage.   However, he sent his
brother Lucius to storm one town, Orinx, which
served Hasdrubal as a strategical pivot from
which to make incursions into the inland States.
This task Lucius carried out successfully, and
Scipio's nature is again instanced in the record
that he commended Lucius with the highest
praise, representing the capture of Orinx as

equal in importance to his own feat at Cartagena. As winter was by now approaching he dismissed the legions to winter quarters, and sent his brother with Hanno and other distinguished prisoners to Rome.

CHAPTER V.

THE BATTLE OF ILIPA.

IN the spring of 206 B.C. the Carthaginians made
their last great effort. Hasdrubal, encouraged
by Mago, Hannibal's brother, raised and armed
fresh levies, and with an army of seventy thousand foot, four thousand horse, and thirty-two
elephants moved north to Ilipa (or Silpia), which
was not far from where Seville stands to-day.
Scipio advanced south from Tarraco to meet the
Carthaginians, collecting auxiliaries at Bæcula
on his way. When he drew near the Bætis and
got fuller information of the opposing force, he
appreciated the formidable nature of the problem.
He felt convinced that with the Roman legions
only he would not be a match for so large an
enemy army, yet to use a large proportion of
allies and rely on their support was to risk the
fate of his father and uncle, whose downfall was
due to the sudden desertion of their allies.
Therefore he decided to use them for the purpose
of impressing and misleading the enemy " by

an imposing show," but leave the main fighting rôle to his own legions. He had learnt, like Wellington two thousand years later, that it was wiser not to place reliance on the co-operation of his Spanish allies. The French in Morocco have imbibed it afresh. Advancing towards Ilipa with a total force, Romans and allies, of forty-five thousand foot and three thousand horse, he came in sight of the Carthaginians, and encamped on certain low hills opposite them. It deserves notice that his advance was on a line which, in the event of victory, would cut them off from the nearest road to Gades, this road running along the south bank of the Bætis river.

Mago, thinking this a favourable chance for a sudden disorganising blow, took most of his cavalry as well as Masinissa with his Numidian horse, and attacked those engaged in forming the camp. But Scipio, as usual, imbued with the principle of security, had foreseen such a possibility, and had posted his own cavalry ready in concealment under shelter of a hill. These charged the forward part of the Carthaginian horse in flank and threw them into disorder, and though the rear echelons, coming up to reinforce the attack, restored the balance for a time, the issue was settled by the sortie of a large body of legionaries from the Roman

camp.   At first the Carthaginians fell back in
good order ; but as the pursuit was vigorously
pressed, they broke up and fled to the shelter
of their own camp.   The result gave Scipio an
initial moral advantage.

The two camps lay facing each other across
a valley between the two low ridges.   For several
successive days Hasdrubal led his army out and
offered battle.   On each occasion Scipio waited
until the Carthaginians were moving out before
he followed suit.   Neither side, however, began
the attack, and towards sundown the two armies,
weary of standing, retired to their camps—the
Carthaginians always first.   One cannot doubt,
in view of the upshot, that on Scipio's side the
delay had a special motive.   On each occasion
also the legions were placed in the Roman centre
opposite to the Carthaginian and African regulars, with the Spanish allies on the wings of
each army.   It became common talk in the
camps that this order of battle was definite, and
Scipio waited until this belief had taken firm
hold.

Then he acted.   He had observed that the
Carthaginians made their daily advance at a late
hour, and had himself purposely waited still
later, to fix this habit on his opponent's mind.
Late in the evening he sent orders through the
camp that the troops should be fed and armed

before daylight, and the cavalry have their horses saddled. Then, while it was scarcely yet daylight, he sent on the cavalry and light troops to attack the enemy's outposts, and himself followed with the legions. This was the first surprise change, and its effect was that the Carthaginians, caught napping by the onset of the Roman cavalry and light troops, had to arm themselves and sally forth without a meal. It further ensured that Hasdrubal would have no time to alter his normal dispositions, even should the idea occur to him. For the second surprise change was that Scipio reversed his former order of battle, and placed the Spanish in his centre and the legions on the wings.

The Roman infantry made no attempt to advance for some hours, the reason for this being Scipio's desire and design to let his hungry opponents feel the effects of their lost breakfast. There was no risk to his other surprise change by so doing, for once drawn up in order of battle the Carthaginians dared not alter their array in face of a watchful and ready opponent. The skirmishing fight between the opposing cavalry and light troops remained indecisive, each when hard-pressed able to take shelter behind their own infantry. Eventually, when Scipio judged the time ripe, he sounded a retreat, and received his skirmishers back through the intervals be-

tween the cohorts, then placing them in reserve behind each wing, the velites behind the
heavy infantry and the cavalry behind the
velites.

It was about the seventh hour[1] when he ordered
the line to advance, but the Spanish centre only
at a slow pace. On arriving within eight hundred yards of the enemy, Scipio, with the right
wing, turned to the right and, wheeling left,
made an oblique advance outwards by successive
cohorts—in column. He had previously sent a
messenger to Silanus and Marcius, commanding
the left wing, to manœuvre similarly. Advancing
rapidly, so that the slow moving centre was
well *refused*, the Roman infantry cohorts wheeled
successively inwards into line as they neared the
enemy, and fell directly on the enemy's flanks,
which but for this manœuvre would have overlapped them. While the heavy infantry thus
pressed the enemy's wings in front, the cavalry
and the velites, under orders, wheeled outwards,
and sweeping round the enemy's flanks took
them in enfilade. This convergent blow on each
wing, sufficiently disruptive because it forced
the defenders to face attack from two directions
simultaneously, was made more decisive in that
it fell on the Spanish irregulars. To add to
Hasdrubal's troubles the cavalry flank attacks

---

[1] The Roman day began at sunrise.

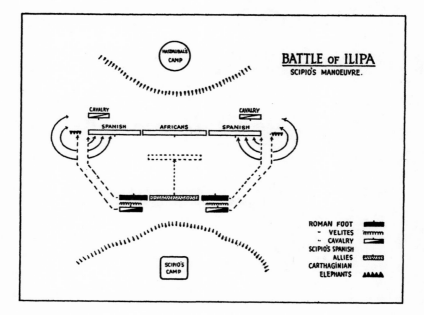

BATTLE of ILIPA
SCIPIO'S MANOEUVRE.

HASDRUBALS CAMP

CAVALRY   CAVALRY
SPANISH   AFRICANS   SPANISH

SCIPIO'S CAMP

ROMAN FOOT
"   VELITES
"   CAVALRY
SCIPIO'S SPANISH
ALLIES
CARTHAGINIAN
ELEPHANTS

drove his elephants, mad with fright, in upon the Carthaginian centre, spreading confusion.

All this time the Carthaginian centre was standing helplessly inactive, unable to help the wings for fear of attack by Scipio's Spaniards, who threatened it without coming to close quarters. Scipio's calculation had enabled him to "fix" the enemy's centre with a minimum expenditure of force, and thus to effect the maximum concentration for his decisive double manœuvre.

Hasdrubal's wings destroyed, the centre, worn out by hunger and fatigue, fell back, at first in good order, but gradually under relentless pressure they broke up, fleeing to their entrenched camp. A drenching downpour, churning the ground in mud under the soldiers' feet, gave them a temporary respite, and prevented the Romans storming the camp on their heels. During the night Hasdrubal evacuated his camp, but as Scipio's strategic advance had placed the Romans across the line of retreat to Gades, he was forced to retire down the western bank towards the Atlantic. Nearly all his Spanish Allies deserted him.

Scipio's light troops were evidently alive to the duty of maintaining contact with the enemy, for he got word from them as soon as it was light of Hasdrubal's departure. He at once followed them up, sending the cavalry ahead, and so rapid was the pursuit that, despite being misled by guides in attempting a short cut to get across Hasdrubal's new line of retreat, the cavalry and velites caught him up. Harassing him continuously, by attacks in flank or in rear, they forced such frequent halts that the legions were able to come up. "After this it was no longer a fight, but a butchering as of cattle," till only Hasdrubal and six thousand half-armed men escaped to the neighbouring hills, out of seventy odd thousand who had fought at Ilipa. The Carthaginians hastily fortified a camp on the highest summit, but though its inaccessibility hindered assault, lack of food caused a constant stream of deserters. At last Hasdrubal left his troops by night, and reaching the sea, not far distant, took ship to Gades, and Mago soon followed him.

Scipio thereupon left Silanus with a force to await the inevitable surrender of the camp, and returned to Tarraco.

Military history contains no more classic example of generalship than this battle of Ilipa. Rarely has so complete a victory been gained by a weaker over a stronger force, and this result was due to a perfect application of the principles of *surprise* and *concentration,* that is in essence an example for all time. How crude does

Frederick's famed oblique order appear beside
Scipio's double oblique manœuvre and envelopment, which effected a crushing concentration
du fort au faible while the enemy's centre was
surely fixed. Scipio left the enemy no chance for
the change of front which cost Frederick so dear
at Kolin. Masterly as were his battle tactics, still
more remarkable perhaps were the decisiveness
and rapidity of their exploitation, which found
no parallel in military history until Napoleon
came to develop the pursuit as the vital com-
plement of battle, and one of the supreme tests
of generalship. To Scipio no cavalry leader
could have complained as Maharbal, whether
justly or not, to Hannibal, "You know, indeed,
how to win a victory, Hannibal, but you know
not how to use one!"

But Scipio, in whom the idea of strategic exploitation was as inborn as the tactical, was not
content to rest on his laurels. Already he was
looking to the future, directing his view on
Africa. As he had seen that Cartagena was the
key to Spain, that Spain was the key to the
situation in Italy, so he saw that Africa was
the key to the whole struggle. Strike at Africa,
and he would not only relieve Italy of Hannibal's
ever-menacing presence—a menace which he had
already reduced by paralysing Hannibal's source
of reinforcement, — but would undermine the

foundations of Carthaginian power, until the edifice itself collapsed in ruin.

To the congratulations of his friends, who entreated him to take a rest, he replied " that he had now to consider how he should begin the war against Carthage ; for up to now the Carthaginians had been making war on the Romans, but now fortune had given the Romans the opportunity of making war on the Carthaginians."

Although it must still be some time before he could convert the Roman Senate to his strategy, he set about preparing the ground. Masinissa, after the defeat at Ilipa, had come over to the Roman side, and was despatched to Africa to induce the Numidians to follow his lead. Further, Scipio sent Lælius on an embassy to sound Syphax, King of the Massæsylians, whose territory embraced most of what is to-day Algeria. Syphax, while expressing his willingness to break with Carthage, refused to ratify any treaty except with Scipio in person.

Though promised a safe conduct, the hazard of such a journey was immense. Diplomatic privileges were then in infancy, and an envoy ran risks, and not infrequently suffered a fate that was enough to chill the stoutest heart. How much greater, too, when the envoy was Rome's one victorious leader, the man whose existence was an ever-growing menace to Car-

thage and her allies, and who was now asked
to entrust himself, far from his army, to the
care of a dubious neutral. Yet this risk Scipio,
calculating the risk against the prize, took, considering that the winning over of Syphax was an
essential step to the further development of his
policy. After making the necessary dispositions
for the protection of Spain, he sailed from Cartagena with two quinqueremes. The risk, as it
proved, was even greater than he calculated.
Indeed, it may be that the history of the ancient
world turned on a puff of wind. For he arrived
off the harbour just after Hasdrubal, driven out
of Spain, had cast anchor there on his way back
to Carthage. Hasdrubal had with him seven
triremes, and sighting the approach of what were
obviously Roman ships, he hurriedly attempted
to prepare his own ships and weigh anchor, in
order to overpower the two quinqueremes before
they could enter the neutral harbour. But a
freshening breeze helped the Roman ships to
enter before Hasdrubal's fleet could sail forth,
and once Scipio was inside the harbour the
Carthaginians did not dare to interfere.

Hasdrubal and Scipio both then sought
audience of Syphax, who was much flattered
by this recognition of his importance. He invited them both to be his guests, and after some
demur they overcame their scruples, and supped

together at Syphax's table. In such a delicate situation, Scipio's personal charm and diplomatic gifts effected a brilliant coup. Not only Syphax but Hasdrubal succumbed to his charm, the Carthaginian openly avowing that Scipio " appeared to him more to be admired for the qualities he displayed on a personal interview with him than for his exploits in war, and that he had no doubt that Syphax and his kingdom were already at the disposal of the Romans, such was the knack that man possessed for gaining the esteem of others." Hasdrubal was a true prophet, for Scipio sailed back with the treaty ratified.

CHAPTER VI.

THE SUBJUGATION OF SPAIN.

SCIPIO had ploughed the ground and sown the seeds for his African campaign. The time for reaping its fruits was not yet, however. He had first to complete the subjugation of Spain, and to deal out punishment to those tribes who had forsaken Rome in her hour of crisis on the Peninsula, after the death of the elder Scipios. Their heir had been too shrewd a diplomatist to show his hand earlier while the scales still hung in the balance, but now, with the Carthaginian power finally broken, it was essential for the future security of the Roman power that such treachery should not pass without retribution. The two chief offenders were Illiturgis and Castulo, cities in the neighbourhood of the battlefield of Bæcula, on the upper reaches of the Bætis (Guadalquiver). Sending a third of his forces under Marcius to deal with Castulo, he himself moved with the remainder on Illiturgis. A guilty conscience is an alert sentinel, and Scipio arrived to find that the Illiturgi had made every preparation for defence without awaiting any declaration of hostilities. He thereupon prepared to assault, dividing his army into two parts, giving command of one to Lælius, in order that they might " attack the city in two places simultaneously, thus creating an alarm in two quarters at the same time " (Livy). Here again it is interesting to note how consistently Scipio executes a convergent assault—his force divided into independently manœuvring parts to effect surprise and strain the enemy's defence, yet combining on a common objective. How strongly does his appreciation of this, the essential formula of tactics, contrast with its rarity in ancient warfare, in modern also, for how often do commanders wreck their plan either on the Scylla of a divided objective or on the Charybdis of a feint or " holding " attack to divert the enemy's attention and reserves from their main blow.

His plan made, Scipio, realising the soldiers' inherently lesser ardour against mere insurgents, strove to stimulate their determination by playing on their feelings for their betrayed comrades. He reminded them that the need for a salutary vengeance ought to make them fight more fiercely than against the Carthaginians. " For with the latter the struggle was for empire and glory almost without any exasperation, while they

had now to punish perfidy and cruelty." Such
an urge was needful, for the men of Illiturgis,
fighting with the courage of despair, with no
hope but to sell their lives as dearly as possible,
repulsed assault after assault. Indeed, because
of the circumstances that Scipio had evidently
foreseen, the previously victorious army "showed
such a want of resolution as was not very honourable to it." At this crisis, Scipio, like Napoleon
at the bridge of Lodi, did not hesitate to stake
his own life. "Considering it incumbent upon
him to exert himself in person and share the
danger, he reproved his soldiers for their cowardice, and ordered the scaling ladders to be brought
up again, threatening to mount the wall himself
since the rest hesitated." "He had now advanced near the walls with no small danger,
when a shout was raised from all sides by the
soldiers, alarmed at the danger to which their
leader was exposed, and the scaling ladders were
raised in several places at once." This fresh
impulse, coinciding with Lælius's pressure elsewhere, turned the scales, and the walls were
captured. During the resultant confusion the
citadel, too, fell to an assault on a side where
it was thought impregnable.

The treachery of Illiturgis was then avenged
in a manner so drastic as to be an object-lesson
of its requital, the inhabitants put to the sword,

and the city itself razed to the ground. Here apparently Scipio made no attempt to restrain the fury of the troops, though, as he was to show on the morrow of Zama, he could be generous beyond comparison to an open foe. In all his acts he evidently envisaged the future, and even in allowing the obliteration of Illiturgis he had a direct purpose. For the news so shook the defenders of Castulo, an obstacle made the more formidable because the garrison had been reinforced by the remains of the Carthaginian forces, that the Spanish commander, throwing over his allies, secretly capitulated. The moral purpose of the Illiturgis sack thus accomplished, Castulo escaped more lightly.

Then, sending Marcius to clear up the few remaining centres of disaffection, Scipio returned to Cartagena to pay his vows to the gods, and to give a gladiatorial show in memory of his father and uncle. This deserves passing mention, for whether due to chance or, as seems more likely, to Scipio's taste, its nature was different from the normal contest. Instead of the gladiators being slaves or captives, doomed to fight " to make a Roman holiday," they were all voluntary and unpaid, either picked representatives of tribes or soldiers anxious to show their prowess in compliment to their general or for desire of glory. Nor were they all of obscure

position, but included several men of distinction,
so that these games at Cartagena might be considered the birthplace of the mediæval tourney.
Some, too, used it as a means to settle personal
disputes, forecasting that still later development,
the duel.

It was shortly after this that deserters arrived
at Cartagena from Gades, offering to betray to
Scipio this last stronghold of the Carthaginian
power in Spain, where Mago had collected ships,
fugitive troops from outlying garrisons in Spain,
and auxiliaries from the African coast across the
straits.   The opportunity was one not to be
missed by Scipio, and he at once despatched
Marcius " with the light cohorts " and Lælius
" with seven triremes and one quinquereme, in
order that they might act in concert by land and
sea " (Livy).   Apart from the light these few
words shed on Scipio's grasp of the advantage of
combined land and sea operations, already made
evident at Cartagena, the specific mention of
" light cohorts " would seem to have a significance.   From Cartagena to Gades is a full four
hundred miles.   To detach light troops, purely,
for a move of this range—a landmark in military
evolution—suggests Scipio's appreciation not only
of the time factor, but also of the advantage of
a highly mobile striking force in situations where
rapidity was the coping-stone on opportunity.

The likelihood also is that he intended to follow with his legions ; but if so, this and his plans in general were upset by a severe illness, which laid him low. Exaggerated by rumour, reports that he was dead soon spread throughout the land, causing such commotion that " neither did the allies keep their allegiance nor the army their duty."

Mandonius and Andobales, dissatisfied because after the expulsion of the Carthaginians the Romans had not obligingly walked out and left them in possession, raised the standard of revolt, and began harassing the territory of the tribes faithful to the Roman alliance. As so often in history, the disappearance of the oppressor was the signal for dependencies to find the presence of their protector irksome. Mandonius and Andobales were but the forerunners of the American colonists and the modern Egyptians. There is no bond so irksome as that of gratitude.

But the menace of the situation was made more acute through the mutiny of the Roman troops themselves at Sucro, midway on the line of communication between Cartagena and Tarraco. It is a truism that line of communication troops are ever the least reliable, the most prone to discontent and disorder. Lack of employment, lack of plunder, were aggravated in this case by lack of pay, which had fallen into arrears. Be-

ginning at first with mere disregard of orders
and neglect of duty, the men soon broke out into
open mutiny, and, driving the tribunes out of
the camp, set up in command two common
soldiers, Albius and Atrius, who had been the
chief instigators of the trouble.

The mutineers had anticipated that with the
general disturbance resulting from Scipio's death,
they would be able to plunder and exact tribute
at will, while escaping notice to a large extent.
But when the rumour of Scipio's death was
refuted, the movement was, if not quenched, at
least damped down. They were in this more
subdued frame of mind when seven military
tribunes arrived, sent by Scipio. These, evidently
under instructions, took a mild line, inquiring
as to their grievances instead of upbraiding them,
and speaking to them by groups rather than
attempting to address an assembly, where the
mob spirit has full play at the expense of reason.

Polybius, and Livy clearly following him, tells
us that Scipio, experienced as he was in war but
not in dealing with sedition, felt great anxiety
and perplexity. If this be so, his course of
action does not suggest it. For a novice, or,
indeed, for a veteran commander, his handling
of the situation was a masterpiece of blended
judgment, tact, and decision. He had sent
collectors round to gather in the contributions

levied on the various cities for the army's maintenance, and took care to let it be known that
this was to adjust the arrears of pay. Then he
issued a proclamation that the soldiers should
come to Carthage to receive their pay, in a body
or in detached parties as they wished. At the
same time he ordered the army at Carthage to
prepare to march against Mandonius and Andobales. These chiefs, incidentally, had withdrawn
within their own borders on hearing that Scipio
was definitely alive. Thus the mutineers on
the one hand felt themselves stripped of possible allies, and on the other, were emboldened
to venture to Cartagena by the prospect of pay
and, still more, of the army's departure. They
took the precaution, however, to come in a body.

The seven tribunes who had inquired into
their grievances were sent to meet them, with
secret instructions to single out the ringleaders,
and invite them to their own quarters to sup.
The mutineers arrived at Cartagena at sunset,
and while encouraged by the sight of the army's
preparations to march, their suspicions were also
lulled by their reception, being greeted as if they
made a timely arrival to relieve the departing
troops. These marched out, according to orders,
at daybreak with their baggage, but on reaching
the gate were halted and their baggage dumped.
Then, promptly, guards were told off to bar all

the exits from the camp, and the rest of the troops to surround the mutineers. Meanwhile the latter had been summoned to an assembly, a summons which they obeyed the more readily because they imagined that the camp, and, indeed, the general himself, were at their mercy.

Their first shock was when they saw their general vigorous and full of health, far from the sick man they had supposed, and their second followed when, after a disconcerting silence, he addressed them in a manner strangely inconsistent with the apparent insecurity of his position. Livy purports to give this speech word for word and at great length, and in his rendering it is a masterpiece of oratory and of style. Polybius's is shorter and crisper, more natural too, and is prefaced by the remark that Scipio " began to speak somewhat as follows." The lover of literature will prefer Livy's version ; but the historian, weighing the evidence of date and circumstance, will prefer to accept Polybius's version, and that as giving the general sense rather than the exact words of Scipio.

Despite these doubts, we will quote Livy for the opening phrases, because they are so telling, and because it is not unlikely that such a beginning might have been recorded with some exactitude. Saying that he was at a loss how to address them, he proceeded : " Can I call you

countrymen, who have revolted from your country ?   Or soldiers, who have rejected the command and authority of your general, and violated
your solemn oath ?   Can I call you enemies ?
I recognise the persons, faces, and dress, and
mien of fellow-countrymen ; but I perceive the
actions, expressions, and intentions of enemies.
For what have you wished and hoped for, but
what the Illitergi and Lacetani did ? "   Next
he expresses wonderment as to what grievance
or what expectations had led them to revolt.
If it is simply a grievance over delays of pay,
caused by his illness, is such action—jeopardising
their country—justified, especially as they have
always been paid in full since he assumed command ?   " Mercenary troops may, indeed, sometimes be pardoned for revolting against their
employers, but no pardon can be extended to
those who are fighting for themselves and their
wives and children.   For that is just as if a man
who said he had been wronged by his own father
over money matters were to take up arms to
kill him who was the author of his life " (Polybius).   If the cause is not merely a grievance,
is it because they hoped for more profit and
plunder by taking service with the enemy ?   If
so, who would be their possible allies ?   Men
like Andobales and Mandonius ; a fine thing to
put their trust in such repeated turncoats !

Then he turns his scorn on the leaders they
have chosen, ignorant and baseborn, parodying
their names, Atrius and Albius—" Blackie " and
" Whitie,"—and so appealing to their sense of
the ridiculous and their superstition. He throws
in a grim reminder of the legion which revolted
at Rhegium, and for it suffered beheading to the
last man. But even these put themselves under
command of a military tribune. What hope of
successful revolt could they have entertained ?
Even had the rumour of his death been correct,
did they imagine that such tried leaders as
Silanus, Lælius, or Scipio's brother could have
failed to avenge the insult to Rome ?

When he has shattered their confidence and
stimulated their fears by such telling arguments,
the way is paved for him to detach them from
the instigators of the revolt and to win back
their loyalty. Changing his tone from harshness
to gentleness, he continues : " I will plead for
you to Rome and to myself, using a plea universally acknowledged among men—that all multi-
tudes are easily misled and easily impelled to
excesses, so that a multitude is ever liable to the
same changes as the sea. For as the sea is by
its own nature harmless to voyagers and quiet,
yet when agitated by winds it appears of the
same turbulent character as the winds, so a multitude ever appears to be and actually is of the

same character as the leaders and counsellors it
happens to have." In Livy's version he makes
also a deftly sympathetic comparison, well calculated to touch their hearts, between his own
recent sickness of body and their sickness of
mind. "Therefore I, too, on the present occasion . . . consent to be reconciled to you, and
grant you an amnesty. But with the guilty
instigators of revolt we refuse to be reconciled,
and have decided to punish for their offences. . . ."
As he finished speaking, the loyal troops, who
had encircled the assembly, clashed their swords
on their shields to strike terror into the mutineers ;
the herald's voice was heard citing by name the
condemned agitators ; and these offenders were
brought bound and naked into the midst of the
assembly, and then executed in the sight of all.
It was a perfectly timed and concerted plan,
and the mutineers were too cowed to raise a
hand or utter a protest. The punishment carried
out, the mass received assurance of forgiveness,
and took a fresh oath of loyalty to the tribunes.
By a characteristic touch of Scipio's, each man
received his full demand of pay as he answered
his name.

This masterly handling of a gravely menacing
situation has more than a reminder of Pétain's
methods in quelling the mutinies of 1917—had
the great Frenchman perchance studied the

mutiny of Sucro ?—not only in its blend of
severity to ringleaders with the just rectification
of grievances, but in the way the moral health
of the body military was restored with the least
possible use of the knife. This was true economy
of force, for it meant that the eight thousand
became not merely unwilling reinforcements,
cowed into acquiescence with orders, but loyal
supporters.

But the suppression of this mutiny was only
one step towards restoring the situation caused
by Scipio's illness. The expedition against
Gades had been abortive, primarily because the
plot had been discovered by the Carthaginian
commander, and the conspirators arrested.
Though they won local successes, Lælius and
Marcius found Gades prepared, and so, forced
to abandon their project, returned to Cartagena.

There Scipio was about to march against the
Spanish rebels. In ten days he reached the
Ebro, a full three hundred miles, and four days
later pitched his camp within sight of the enemy.
A circular valley lay between the two camps,
and into this he drove some cattle protected only
by light troops, to " excite the rapacity of the
barbarians." At the same time he placed Lælius
with the cavalry in concealment behind a spur.
The bait succeeded, and while the rival skirmishers
were merrily engaged, Lælius emerged from cover,

part of his cavalry charging the Spanish in front,
and the other part riding round the foot of the
hill to cut them off from their camp. The con-
sequent reverse so irritated the Spanish that
next morning at daybreak their army marched
out to offer battle.

This suited Scipio excellently, for the valley
was so confined that the Spanish by this act committed themselves to a cramped close quarter
combat on the level, where the peculiar aptitude
of the Romans in hand-to-hand fighting gave
them an initial advantage over troops more
adapted to hill fighting at longer ranges. And,
furthermore, in order to find room for their horse
they were forced to leave one-third of their foot
out of the battle, stationed on the slope behind.

The conditions suggested a fresh expedient to
Scipio. The valley was so narrow that the
Spanish could not post their cavalry on the
flanks of the infantry line, which took up the
whole space. Seeing this, Scipio realised that
his own infantry flanks were automatically
secured, and accordingly sent Lælius with the
cavalry round by the hills in a wide turning
movement. Then, ever alive to the vital importance of securing his intended manœuvre by
a vigorous fixing attack, he himself advanced
into the valley with his infantry, with four
cohorts in front, this being the most he could

effectively deploy on the narrow front. This
thrust, as he intended, occupied the attention of
the Spanish, and prevented them from observing the cavalry manœuvre until the blow fell,
and they heard the noise of the cavalry engagement in their rear. Thus the Spanish were forced
to fight two separate battles, their cavalry
neither able to aid their infantry, nor the infantry their cavalry, and each doomed to the
demoralising sound of conflict in their rear, so
that each action had a moral reaction on the
other.

Cramped and assailed by skilled close-quarter
fighters, whose formation gave them the advantage of depth for successive blows, the Spanish
infantry were cut to pieces. Then the Spanish
cavalry, surrounded, suffering the pressure of
the fugitives, the direct attack of the Roman
infantry, and the rear attack of the Roman
cavalry, could not use their mobility, and, forced
to a standing fight, were slain to the last man
after a gallant but hopeless resistance. It is a
testimony to the fierceness of the fight and to
the quality of the Spanish resistance, when hope
had gone, that the Roman losses were twelve
hundred killed and over three thousand wounded.
Of the Spanish the only survivors were the light-
armed third of their force who had remained on
the hill, idle spectators of the tragedy in the

valley.   These, along with their chiefs, fled in time.

This decisive triumph was a fitting conclusion to Scipio's Spanish campaigns—campaigns which for all their long neglect by military students reveal a profound grasp of strategy—at a time when strategy had hardly been born,—and of its intimate relation to policy.   But, above all, they deserve to be immortalised for their richness of tactical achievement.   Military history hardly contains such another series of ingenious and inspired battle manœuvres, surpassing on balance even those of Hannibal in Italy.   If Scipio profited by Hannibal's unintended course of instruction on the battlefields of Italy, the pupil surpassed even the master.   Nor does such a probability diminish Scipio's credit, for the highest part of the art of war is inborn, not acquired, or why did not later captains, ancient and modern, profit more by Scipio's demonstrations.   Wonderful as was Hannibal's fertility of plan, there appears in Scipio's record a still richer variety, a still more complete calculation, and in three directions a definite superiority. The attack on a fortified place was admittedly in Hannibal a weakness ; in Scipio the reverse, for Cartagena is a landmark in history.   The pursuit after Ilipa marks a new advance in warfare, as also the wide concealed turning movement in this last battle against Andobales, a development clearly beyond the narrow outflanking manœuvres which had hitherto been the high-water mark of tactical skill.

Scipio's military motto would seem to have been "every time a new stratagem." Has ever a general been so fertile an artist of war? Beside him most of the celebrated captains of history appear mere dabblers in the art, showing in their whole career but one or two variations of orthodox practice. And be it remembered that with one exception Scipio's triumphs were won over first-class opponents ; not, like Alexander, over Asiatic mobs; like Cæsar, over tribal hordes; or like Frederick and Napoleon, over the courtier-generals and senile pedants of an atrophied military system.

This victory over Andobales and Mandonius proved to be the coping-stone not only on his military career in Spain, but on the political conquest of the country. So decisive had it been that Andobales realised the futility of further resistance, and sent his brother Mandonius to sue for peace unconditionally. One imagines that Mandonius must have felt some pessimism as to his reception and as to his tenure of life. It would have been natural to have dealt out to these twice-repeated rebels a dire vengeance. But Scipio knew human nature, including Spanish nature. No vengeance could improve his military or political position, now unchallenged, whereas, on the other hand, it would merely sow the seeds of future trouble, convert the survivors into embittered foes, biding their time for a fresh outbreak. Little as he counted on their fidelity, generosity was the one course which might secure it. Therefore, after upbraiding Mandonius, and through him, Andobales, driving home the helplessness of their position and the rightful forfeiture of their lives, he made a peace as generous as it was diplomatically foresighted. To show how little he feared them, he did not demand the surrender of their arms and all their possessions, as was the custom, nor even the required hostages, saying that " should they revolt, he would not take vengeance on their unoffending hostages, but upon themselves, inflicting punishment not upon defenceless but on armed enemies " (Livy). The wisdom of this policy found its justification in the fact that from this juncture Spain disappears from the history of the Punic War, whether as a base of recruitment and supply for the Carthaginian armies or as a distraction from Scipio's concentration on his new objective —Carthage itself. True, revolts broke out at intervals, the first avowedly from the contempt

felt by the Spanish for the generals who succeeded Scipio, and recurred for centuries. But
they were isolated and spasmodic outbursts, and
limited to the hill tribes, in whose blood fighting
was a malarial fever.

Scipio's mission in Spain was accomplished.
Only Gades held out as the last fragment of the
Carthaginian power, and this, being then an
island fortress, was impregnable save through
possible betrayal by its defenders. By some
historians Mago's escape from Gades is made
an imputation on Scipio's generalship, yet from
a comparison of the authorities it would seem
probable that Mago left there, under orders from
Carthage, while Scipio was occupied with the
far more pressing menace of the mutiny and
Andobales's revolt. Mago, too, was not such a
redoubtable personality that his departure, with
a handful of troops, for other fields was in itself
a menace to the general situation, even if it
could have been prevented, which militarily was
impossible. Actually, on his voyage from Gades,
he attempted a surprise assault on Cartagena in
the absence of Scipio, and was so easily repulsed
and so strongly counter-attacked, that the ships
cut their anchors in order to avoid being boarded,
leaving many of the defeated soldiers to drown
or be slain. Forced to return to Gades to recruit

afresh, he was refused entry to the city by the
inhabitants, who shortly surrendered to the
Romans, and had to retrace his course to the
island of Pityusa (modern Iviça), the western-
most of the Balearic Isles, which was inhabited
by Carthaginians. After receiving recruits and
supplies, he attempted a landing on Majorca,
but was repulsed by the natives, famous as
slingers, and had to choose the less advantageous
site of Minorca as his winter quarters, there
hauling his ships on shore.

With regard to the chronology of this last
phase, in Livy's account the suppression of
Andobales's rebellion is followed by the story
of a meeting between Scipio and Masinissa, and
then by the details of Mago's departure from
Gades, from which it would appear that this
happened while Scipio was still in Spain. But
for accuracy of historical sequence Livy is a less
reliable guide than Polybius, and the latter's
narrative definitely states that directly after the
subjugation of Andobales Scipio returned to
Tarraco, and then, "anxious not to arrive in
Rome too late for the consular elections," sailed
for Rome, after handing over the army to Silanus
and Marcius, and arranging for the administration of the province.

The meeting with Masinissa, whenever it occurred, is worth notice, for here the seeds of Scipio's generous treatment of Masinissa's nephew years before bore fruit in the exchange of pledges of an alliance, which was to be one of Scipio's master-tools in undermining the Carthaginian power at its base in Africa.

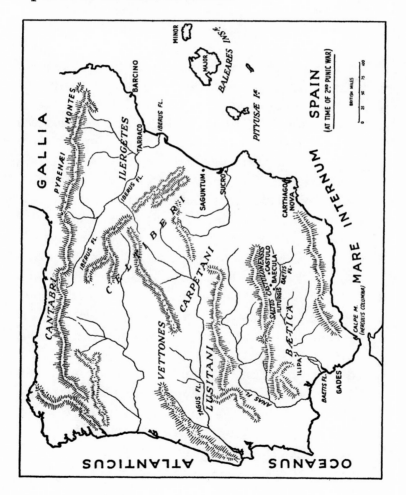

CHAPTER VII.

THE TRUE OBJECTIVE.

ON arrival at Rome Scipio obtained an audience
of the Senate outside the city, at the temple of
Bellona, and there gave them a formal report
of his campaigns. " On account of these services
he rather tried his prospect of a triumph than
pressed it pertinaciously," for the honour had
never been given except to those whose services
were rendered when holders of a magistracy.
His tact was wise, for the astonishing success of
youth had already inspired envy among his
seniors. The Senate did not break with prece-
dent, and at the close of the audience he entered
the city in the ordinary way. His reward, however, came without delay. At the assembly for
the election of the two consuls for the coming
year he was named by all the centuries. The
popularity of his election was shown not only
by the enthusiasm which greeted it, but by the
gathering of a larger number of voters than at
any time during the Punic War, crowds swarm-

ing to his house and to the Capitol full of curi-
osity to see the victor of the Spanish wars.

But on the morrow of this personal triumph,
compensation for the formal " triumph " denied
him by a hidebound Senate, the first shoots
appeared of that undergrowth of narrow-minded
conservatism, reinforced by envy, which was to
choke the personal fruits of his work, though
happily not before he had garnered for Rome
the first-fruits—Hannibal's overthrow.

Hitherto in Spain he had enjoyed a free hand
unfettered by jealous politicians or the compro-
mising counsels of government by committee.
If he had to rely on his own local resources, he
was at least too far distant for his essential freedom of action to be controlled by any many-
headed guardian of national policy. But from
now on he was to suffer, like Marlborough and
Wellington some two thousand years later, the
curb of political faction and jealousy, and finally,
like Marlborough, end his days in embittered
retirement. The report got about that he was
saying that he had been declared consul not
merely to prosecute, but to finish the war ; that
for this object it was essential for him to move
with his army into Africa ; and that if the
Senate opposed this plan he would carry it
through with the people's backing, overriding
the Senate. Perhaps his friends were indis-

creet; perhaps Scipio himself, so old beyond his years in other ways, allowed youthful confidence to outride his discretion; perhaps, most probable of all, he knew the Senate's innate narrowness of vision and had been sounding the people's opinion.

The upshot was, that when the question was raised in the Senate, Fabius Cunctator voiced the conservative view. The man who had worthily won his name by inaction, his natural caution reinforced by an old man's jealousy, cleverly if spitefully criticises the plan of a young man whose action threatens to eclipse his fame. First, he points out that neither had the Senate voted nor the people ordered that Africa should be constituted a consul's province this year, insinuating that if the consul came before them with his mind already made up, such conduct is an insult to them. Next, Fabius seeks to parry any imputation of jealousy by dwelling on his own past achievements as if they were too exalted for any possible feats of Scipio to threaten comparison. How characteristic, too, of age the remark, "What rivalry can there exist between myself and a man who is not equal in years even to my son?" He urges that Scipio's duty is to attack Hannibal in Italy. "Why do you not apply yourself to this, and carry the war in a straightforward manner to the place where Han-

nibal is, rather than pursue that roundabout
course, according to which you expect that when
you have crossed into Africa Hannibal will follow
you thither." How vivid is the reminder here
of Eastern *v.* Western controversy in the war of
1914-1918. "What if Hannibal should advance
against Rome ? " How familiar to modern ears
is this argument employed against any military
heretic who questions the doctrine of Clausewitz
that the enemy's main army is the primary
military objective.

Fabius then insinuates that Scipio's head has
been turned by his successes in Spain. These
Fabius damns with faint praise and covert sneers
—sneers which Mommsen and other modern
historians seem to have accepted as literal truth,
forgetting how decisively all Fabius's arguments
were refuted by Scipio's actions. How different,
Fabius contends, is the problem Scipio will have
to face if he ventures to Africa. Not a harbour
open, not even a foothold already secured, not
an ally. Does Scipio trust his hold over Masinissa when he could not trust even his own
soldiers ?—a jibe at the Sucro mutiny. Land in
Africa, and he will rally the whole land against
him, all internal disputes forgotten in face of
the foreign foe. Even in the unlikely event of
forcing Hannibal's return, how much worse will
it be to face him near Carthage, supported by all

Africa, instead of with a remnant in Southern
Italy ?   " What sort of policy is that of yours,
to prefer fighting where your own forces will be
diminished by one-half, and the enemy's greatly
augmented ? "

Fabius finishes with a scathing comparison of
Scipio with his father, who, setting out for Spain,
returned to Italy to meet Hannibal, " while you
are going to leave Italy when Hannibal is there,
not because you consider such a course beneficial
to the State, but because you think it will re-
dound to your honour and glory . . . the armies
were enlisted for the protection of the city and
of Italy, and not for the consuls, like kings, to
carry into whatever part of the world they please
from motives of vanity."

This speech makes a strong impression on the
Senators, " especially those advanced in years,"
and when Scipio rises to reply the majority are
clearly against him.   His opening is an apt
counter-thrust :   " Even Quintus Fabius himself
has observed . . . that in the opinion he gave a
feeling of jealousy might be suspected.   And
though I dare not myself charge so great a man
with harbouring that feeling, yet, whether it is
owing to a defect in his phrasing, or to the fact,
that suspicion has certainly not been removed.
For he has so magnified his own honours and
the fame of his exploits, to do away with the

imputation of envy, that it would appear I am
in danger of being rivalled by every obscure person, but not by himself, because he enjoys an
eminence above everybody else. . . ." " He has
represented himself as an old man, and as one
who has gone through every gradation of honour,
and me as below the age even of his son, as if
he supposed that the desire of glory did not
exceed the span of life, and as if its chief part
had no respect to memory and future ages."
Then, with gentle sarcasm Scipio refers to Fabius's
expressed solicitude for his safety, and not only
for the army and the State, should he cross over
to Africa. Whence has this concern so suddenly
sprung ? When his father and uncle were slain,
when Spain lay beneath the heel of four victorious Carthaginian armies, when no one except himself would offer themselves for such a
forlorn venture, " why was it that no one at
that time made any mention of my age, of the
strength of the enemy, of the difficulties, of the
recent fate of my father and uncle ? " " Are
there now larger armies in Africa, more and
better generals, than were then in Spain ? Was
my age then more mature for conducting a war
than now . . .? " " After having routed four
Carthaginian armies . . . after having regained
possession of the whole of Spain, so that no
trace of war remains, it is an easy matter to

make light of my services; just as easy as it would be, should I return from Africa, to make light of those very conditions which are now magnified for the purpose of detaining me here." Then, after demolishing the historical examples which Fabius had quoted as warnings, Scipio makes this appeal to history recoil against Fabius by adducing Hannibal's example in support of his plan. " He who brings danger upon another has more spirit than he who repels it. Add to this, that the terror excited by the unexpected is increased thereby. When you have entered the territory of an enemy you obtain a near view of his strong and weak points." After pointing out the moral " soft spots " in Africa, Scipio continues : " Provided no impediment is caused here, you will hear at once that I have landed, and that Africa is blazing with war; that Hannibal is preparing to depart from this country." ". . . Many things which are not now apparent at this distance will develop; and it is the part of a general not to be wanting when opportunity arises, and to bend its events to his designs. I shall, Quintus Fabius, have the opponent you assign me, Hannibal, but I shall rather draw him after me than be kept here by him." As for the danger of a move by Hannibal on Rome, it is a poor compliment to Crassus, the other consul, to suppose that

he will not be able to keep Hannibal's reduced
and shaken forces in check, when Fabius did so
with Hannibal at the height of his power and
success—an unanswerable master-thrust this !

After emphasising that now is the time and
the opportunity to turn the tables on Carthage,
to do to Africa what Hannibal did to Italy,
Scipio ends on a characteristic note of restraint
and exaltation combined : " Though Fabius has
depreciated my services in Spain, I will not
attempt to turn his glory into ridicule and
magnify my own. If in nothing else, though
a young man, I will show my superiority over
this old man in modesty and in the government
of my tongue. Such has been my life, and such
the services I have performed, that I can rest
content in silence with that opinion which you
have spontaneously formed of me."

The Senate, however, were more concerned
with the preservation of their own privileges
than with the military arguments, and demanded
to know if Scipio would leave the decision with
them, or, if they refused, appeal, over their
heads, to the people's verdict. They refused to
give a decision until they had an assurance that
he would abide by it. After a consultation with
his colleague, Scipio gave way to this demand.
Thereupon the Senate, a typical committee,
effected a compromise by which the consul to

whose lot Sicily fell might have permission to
cross into Africa if he judged it to be for the
advantage of the State. Curiously, Sicily fell to
Scipio !

He took with him thirty warships, which by
great energy he had built and launched within
forty-five days of the timber being taken from
the woods ; of these twenty were quinqueremes
and ten quadriremes. On board he embarked
seven thousand volunteers, as the Senate, afraid
to block him but keen to obstruct him, had
refused him leave to levy troops.

The story of how, beset with difficulties and
hampered by those he was aiming to save, he
took this unorganised band of volunteers and
trained it to be the nucleus of an effective expeditionary force finds a notable parallel in our own
history. Sicily was to be Scipio's Shorncliffe
Camp, the place where he forged the weapon
that was to be thrust at the heart of Carthage.
But Scipio, unlike Sir John Moore in the Napo-
leonic War, was himself to handle the weapon
his genius had created, and with it to strike the
death-blow at Hannibal's power. His vision
penetrating the distant future, a quality in which
he perhaps surpasses all other great commanders,
enabled him to realise that the tactical key to
victory lay in the possession of a superior mobile
arm of decision—cavalry. It is not the least

tribute to his genius that to appreciate this he
had to break loose from the fetters of a great
tradition, for Rome's military greatness was
essentially built on the power of her legionary
infantry. The long and splendid annals of
Roman history are the testimony to its effective-
ness, and only in Scipio's brief passage across the
stage do we find a real break with this tradition,
a balance between the two arms by which the
power of the one for fixing and of the other for
decisive manœuvre are proportioned and combined. It is an object-lesson to modern general
staffs, shivering on the brink of mechanicalisa-
tion, fearful of the plunge despite the proved
ineffectiveness of the older arms in their present
form, for no military tradition has been a tithe
so enduring and so resplendent as that of
the legion. From his arrival in Sicily onwards
Scipio bent his energies to developing a superior
cavalry, and Zama, where Hannibal's decisive
weapon was turned against himself, is Scipio's
justification.

How unattainable must this goal have seemed
when he landed in Sicily with a mere seven thousand heterogeneous volunteers. Yet within a
few days the first progress was recorded. At
once organising his volunteers into cohorts and
centuries, Scipio kept aside three hundred of
the pick. One can imagine their perplexed

wonder at being left without arms and not told off to centuries like their comrades.

Next he nominated three hundred of the noblest born Sicilian youths to accompany him to Africa, and appointed a day on which they were to present themselves equipped with horses and arms. The honour of nomination for such a hazardous venture affrighted both them and their parents, and they paraded most reluctantly. Addressing them, Scipio remarked that he had heard rumours of their aversion to this arduous service, and rather than take unwilling comrades he would prefer that they would openly avow their feelings. One of them immediately seized this loophole of escape, and Scipio thereupon released him from service and promised to provide a substitute on condition that he handed over his horse and arms and trained his substitute in their handling. The Sicilian joyfully accepted, and the rest, seeing that the general did not take his action amiss, promptly followed his example. By this means Scipio obtained a nucleus of picked Roman cavalry " at no expense to the State."

His next measures show not only how his every step tended towards his ultimate object, but also how alive he was to the importance of foresight in securing his future action. He sent Lælius on an advance reconnoitring expedi-

tion to Africa, and in order not to impair the
resources he was building up repaired his old
ships for this expedition, hauling his new ones
upon shore for the winter at Panormus, as they
had been hastily and inevitably built of un-
seasoned timber. Further, after distributing his
army through the towns, he ordered the Sicilian
States to furnish corn for the troops, saving up
the corn which he had brought with him from
Italy—economy of force even in the details of
supply. Scipio knew that strategy depends on
supply, that without security of food the most
dazzling manœuvres may come to nought.

Furthermore, an offensive, whether strategical
or tactical, must operate from a secure base—
this is one of the cardinal axioms of war. " Basis "
would perhaps be a better term, for " base " is
apt to be construed too narrowly, whereas truly
it comprises security to the geographical base,
both internal and external, as well as security
of supply and of movement. Napoleon in 1814,
the Germans in 1918, both suffered the disloca-
tion of their offensive action through the insecurity of their base internally. It is thus
interesting to note how Scipio sought among
his preparatory measures to ensure this security.
He found Sicily, and especially Syracuse, suffering
from internal discontent and disorder which had
arisen out of the war. The property of the

Syracusans had been seized after the famous
siege by covetous Romans and Italians, and
despite the decrees of the Senate for its restitution, had never been handed back. Scipio took
an early opportunity of going to Syracuse, and
" deeming it of the first importance to maintain
trust in Rome's plighted word," restored their
property to the citizens, by proclamation and
even by direct action against those who still
clung fast to the plundered property. This act
of justice had a wide effect throughout Sicily,
and not only ensured the tranquillity of his base
but won the active support of the Sicilians in
furnishing his forces for the expedition.

Meanwhile Lælius had landed at Hippo Regius
(modern Bona), about 150 miles distant from
Carthage. According to Livy the news threw
Carthage into a panic, the citizens believing that
Scipio himself had landed with his army, and
anticipating an immediate march on Carthage.
To ward this off seemed hopeless, as their own
people were untrained for war, their mercenary
troops of doubtful loyalty, and among the African
chiefs Syphax was alienated from them since his
conference with Scipio, and Masinissa a declared
enemy. The panic did not abate until news came
that the invader was Lælius, not Scipio, and that
his forces were only strong enough for a raid.
Livy further tells us that the Carthaginians took

advantage of the respite to send embassies to
Syphax and others of the African chiefs for the
purpose of strengthening their alliance, and
envoys were also sent to Hannibal and Mago to
urge them to keep Scipio at home by playing
on the fears of the Romans. Mago had, earlier,
landed at Genoa, but was too weak to act effectively, and to encourage him to move towards
Rome and join Hannibal, the Carthaginian Senate
sent him seven thousand troops and also money
to hire auxiliaries.

If these facts be true, they would on the
surface suggest that Scipio lost an opportunity
and was unwise to put the Carthaginians on
their guard by this raid of Lælius's, and this
impression is strengthened by the words ascribed
to Masinissa. For Livy says that Masinissa came,
with a small body of horse, to meet Lælius,
and complained that " Scipio had not acted
with promptness, in that he had not already
passed his army over into Africa, while the
Carthaginians were in consternation, and while
Syphax was entangled in wars with neighbouring
States, and in doubt as to the side he should
take ; that if Syphax was allowed time to settle
his own affairs, he would not keep faith with
the Romans." Masinissa then begged that
Lælius would urge Scipio not to delay, promis-
ing that he, though driven from his kingdom,

would join Scipio with a force of horse and foot.

When, however, we appreciate the situation from a military angle it appears in a different light. Lælius landed at the port which was nearest to Numidia, and which was not only 150 miles distant from Carthage, but with a wide belt of hill country intervening. When Scipio himself landed it was at a spot only some twenty-five miles distant. Hence Lælius's expedition can have been in no sense a reconnaissance against Carthage, and the clear deduction is that it was a reconnaissance to discover the state and feeling of the African States where Scipio hoped to find allies, and in particular to get in touch with Masinissa. As we have shown, Scipio had realised that a superiority in the cavalry arm was the key to victory over the Carthaginians, and he looked to the Numidian chief for his main source. His appreciation of the latter's brilliant cavalry leadership on the battlefields of Spain had inspired him to win Masinissa over. Thus the inherent probability is that Lælius's mission was primarily to discover if the Numidian would actually hold to his new alliance when Roman troops landed on African soil, and if so, what were the resources he could contribute. If the Carthaginians were really panic-stricken at a raid so distant, the fact but

helped to confirm Scipio's view of the moral
advantage to be gained from a thrust at Carthage.
As for the warning thus given, the danger of
putting the Carthaginians on their guard, this
had already been given by Scipio's speeches in
the Senate and his preparations. Where consent
for his expedition had to be wrung from a reluc-
tant Senate, where the forces and resources for
it had to be raised without State help, strategic
surprise was out of the question from the outset.
Here were exemplified the chronic drawbacks of
a constitutional system of government for conducting war. It is one of Scipio's supreme merits
that he obtained completely decisive results,
though lacking the tremendous asset of political
control. He, the servant of a republic, is the
one exception to the rule that throughout the
history of war the most successful of the great
captains have been despots or autocrats. Count-
less historians have lavished sympathy on Hannibal for the handicap he suffered through lack
of support from home, and laid all his set-backs
at the door of the Carthaginian Senate. None
seem to have stressed Scipio's similar handicap.
Yet to Rome there was none of the physical
difficulty in sending reinforcements that Carthage
could plead as an excuse. In this lack of support—nay worse, the active opposition—from the
Roman Senate lies unquestionably the reason

of Scipio's delay of a year in Sicily to prepare
for the expedition. He had to find unaided his
own resources in Sicily and Africa. How ground-
less as well as irrational was Masinissa's complaint, if he made it, is shown by the fact that
when, in 204 B.C., Scipio landed in Africa, the
" landless prince," to quote Mommsen, " brought
in the first instance nothing beyond his personal
ability to the aid of the Romans." Few generals
have been so bold as Scipio when boldness was
the right policy, but he was too imbued with
the principle of security to strike before he had
armed himself and tempered his weapon by
training. The wonder is not at Scipio's delay
of a year, but that he moved so soon, and with
a force that in numbers if not in training was
still so puny for the scope of his task. But this
seeming audacity was made secure by his strategy
after the landing, and Zama was its justification.
It is an ironical comment on the value of their
judgments that the same historians who criticise
Scipio for his tardiness in 205 B.C., tax him with
rashness for the smallness of the force with
which he sailed in 204 B.C. ! One of these, Dodge,
when dealing with the first year, remarks that
" Scipio does not seem to have been very expedi-
tious about the business. In this he resembled
M'Clellan, as well as in his popularity." Later,

dealing with Scipio's embarkation, Dodge says:
" Some generals would have declared these means
insufficient ; but Scipio possessed an abundance
of self-confidence which supplemented material
strength in all but severe tests." Such criticism
is a boomerang recoiling on the critic.

CHAPTER VIII.

A POLITICAL HITCH.

THE interval between the return of Lælius and
the embarkation for Africa is occupied, apart
from material preparation, by two episodes of
significance. The first is Scipio's apparent "side-
show" at Locri; the second, the political im-
broglio which for a time threatened his ruin and
that of his plans. Both deserve study for the
light they shed on his character as a commander
and a man.

Locri lay on the underpart of the toe of Italy
(near modern Gerace), and was in Hannibal's
possession. After his brother Hasdrubal's defeat
at the Metaurus, Hannibal had fallen back on
Bruttium, the southernmost province of Italy,
and here he held at bay the consular armies,
who dared not advance to seek out the scarred
but indomitable lion in his mountain fastnesses.

Some Locrians who had gone outside the walls
were captured by a Roman raiding party, and
taken to Rhegium—the port adjacent to Sicily,—

where they were recognised by the pro-Roman
Locrian nobles, who had found sanctuary there
when their town fell into Carthaginian hands.
Certain of the prisoners, who were skilled artisans
and had been in the employment and trust of
the Carthaginians, suggested that, if ransomed,
they would be willing to betray the citadel at
Locri. The nobles, eager to regain their town,
at once ransomed the artisans, and after con-
certing a plan and signals, sent them back to
Locri. Then, going to Scipio at Syracuse, they
told him of the scheme. He saw the opportunity,
and despatched on the venture a detachment of
three thousand men under two military tribunes.
Exchanging signals with the conspirators inside,
ladders were let down about midnight, and the
attackers swarmed up the walls. Surprise magnified their strength, and the Carthaginians in
confusion fled from the citadel to a second citadel
on the farther side of the town. For several
days encounters occurred between the two parties
without decisive result. Alive to the danger to
his garrison, and to the threatened loss of an
important point, Hannibal moved to the rescue,
sending a messenger ahead with orders to the
garrison to make a sortie at daybreak as a cloak
to what he hoped would be his surprise assault.
He had not, however, brought scaling ladders
with him, and so was forced to postpone his

attack a day while he was preparing these and
other materials for storming the walls.

Scipio, who was at Messana, received word
of Hannibal's move, and planned a counter-
surprise. Leaving his brother in command at
Messana, he embarked a force, and, setting sail
on the next tide, arrived in the harbour of
Locri shortly before nightfall. The troops were
hidden in the town during the night, a concealment made possible by the townspeople favour-
ing, though not openly taking, the side of the
Romans. Next morning Hannibal launched his
assault in conjunction with the sortie from the
Carthaginians' citadel. As the scaling ladders
were being brought forward, Scipio sallied out
from one of the town gates and attacked the
Carthaginians in flank and rear. The shock of
the surprise dislocated and disorganised the
Carthaginians, and, his plan upset, Hannibal fell
back on his own camp. Realising that the
Romans, because of their grip on the town, were
masters of the situation, he withdrew during
the night, sending word to his garrison in the
citadel to make their way out as best they could
and rejoin him.

For Scipio this " side-show " was a very real
asset. Apart from the personal prestige he gained
from his success in this first encounter with the
dreaded Hannibal, scoring a trick even off the

master of ruses, he had helped the Roman campaign in Italy by curtailing Hannibal's remaining foothold in that country—and without any diminution of his own force. But, beyond these personal and indirect gains, his success had an important bearing on his own future plan of operations. For he had " blooded " his troops against Hannibal, and by this successful enterprise given them a moral tonic, which would be of immense value in the crucial days to come. It is unfortunate that for this episode, as for Lælius's reconnaissance in Africa, we have no Polybius to reveal to us the motives and calculations which inspired Scipio's moves. The loss of Polybius's books on this period must be replaced by deduction from the facts, and from the knowledge already gained of Scipio's mind. To those who have followed his constant and far-sighted exploitation of the moral element during his Spanish campaigns, there can be little doubt that he seized on the Locri expedition as a heaven-sent chance not only to test and sharpen his weapon for the day of trial, but to dispel in his troops the impression of Hannibalic invincibility.

The second episode arose out of the subsequent administration of recaptured Locri. When Scipio had sent the original force to seize the town, he had instructed Quintus Pleminius, the propraetor at Rhegium, to assist the tribunes, and

when the place was captured Pleminius, by
virtue of his seniority, assumed the command
until Scipio arrived. After the repulse of Hannibal's relieving force, Scipio returned to Sicily,
and Pleminius was naturally left in chief command of the town and its defence, though the
detachment from Sicily remained under the
direct command of the tribunes.

How Pleminius abused his trust is one of the
most sordid pages in Roman history. The
wretched inhabitants suffered worse from his
tyranny and lust than ever they had from the
Carthaginians—an ill-requital of their aid to
the Romans in regaining the town. The example
of their leader infected the troops, and their
greed for loot not only harassed the townspeople
but inevitably led to disorder among themselves.
It would seem that the tribunes strove to check
this growing license, and to uphold the true
standards of military discipline. One of Pleminius's men, running away with a silver cup that
he had stolen from a house and pursued by its
owners, met the tribunes in his flight. They
stopped him and had the cup taken away, whereat
his comrades showered abuse on the tribunes,
and the disturbance soon ended in a free fight
between the soldiers of the tribunes and those of
Pleminius. The latter were worsted and invoked
the aid of their commander, inciting him by

tales of the reproaches cast upon his behaviour and control. Pleminius thereupon ordered the tribunes to be brought before him, stripped, and beaten. During the short delay while the rods were being brought and themselves stripped, the tribunes called upon their men for aid. The latter, hastily gathering from all quarters, were so inflamed at the sight that, breaking loose from the habits of discipline, they vented their rage on Pleminius. Cutting him off from his party, they mutilated his nose and ears, and left him almost lifeless.

When word of the disturbance reached Scipio, he sailed immediately for Locri and held a court of inquiry. Of the evidence and of the reasons for his judgment we know nothing. All that is handed down is the fact that he acquitted Pleminius, restored him to command, and pronouncing the tribunes guilty, ordered them to be thrown into chains and sent back to Rome for the Senate to deal with. He then returned to Sicily.

The verdict appears somewhat astonishing, the one serious blemish, in fact, on Scipio's judgment. The motives which inspired it are difficult to surmise. Perhaps it was partly pity for the mutilated Pleminius, combined with anger that his own men should have shown such gross insubordination and committed such an atrocity.

It is a natural instinct with the best type of commander to be more severe on the misconduct of his own direct subordinates than on those who are only attached to him, and in case of dispute between the two such a man may err because of his very scrupulousness to hold the balance fairly, and to avoid partiality towards his own. It was said of one of the finest British commanders in the war of 1914-18 that if he had a personal dislike or distrust of a subordinate he invariably gave the latter more rope than the others, knowing that if his distrust was justified the man would assuredly use this rope to hang himself. Similar may have been the motives underlying Scipio's outwardly inexplicable verdict. In criticising it the historian must consider not only the gaps in our knowledge of the case, but view the incident in the general light of all Scipio's recorded acts as a commander. The whole weight of evidence, as we have seen, goes to show that two qualities which especially distinguished Scipio were the acuteness of his understanding of men, and his humanity to the conquered. Trust in a Pleminius or condonation of brutality were the last things to be expected of him, and so, lacking evidence as to the facts on which his decision was based, it would be rash to pass adverse judgment on his action.

We need to remember also that Locri was in

Italy, and therefore outside his province, and a close attention to its administration could only be at the expense of his primary object—preparation for the expedition to Africa.

The importance of the Locri incident is not as a light on Scipio's character, but as a political rock on which his military plans nearly foundered. How this came about can be briefly told. After Scipio's departure, Pleminius, who thought that the injury he had sustained had been treated too lightly by Scipio, disobeyed the latter's instructions. He had the tribunes dragged before him and tortured to death, refusing even to allow their mangled bodies to be buried. His injuries still rankling, he then sought to avenge himself by multiplying the burdens put on the Locrians. In despair, they sent a deputation to the Roman Senate. Their envoys arrived soon after the consular elections, which had marked the end of Scipio's term of office, though he was continued in command of the troops in Sicily. Their tale of misery raised a storm of popular indignation at Rome, and Scipio's senatorial opponents were not slow to divert this on to the head of the man nominally responsible. It is no surprise to find that Fabius initiated this by asking if they had carried their complaints to Scipio. The envoys replied, according to Livy, that "deputies were sent to him, but he was occupied with the preparations for the war, and had either already crossed over into Africa, or was on the point of doing so." They added that his previous decision between Pleminius and the tribunes had given them the impression that the former was in favour with Scipio.

Fabius had got the answer he wanted, and after the envoys had withdrawn, hastened to condemn Scipio unheard, declaring "that he was born for the corruption of military discipline. In Spain he almost lost more men in consequence of the mutiny than in the war. That, after the manner of foreigners and kings, he indulged the licentiousness of the soldiers, and then punished them with cruelty." This envenomed speech Fabius followed up with " a resolution equally harsh." It was "that Pleminius should be conveyed to Rome in chains, and in chains plead his cause; that, if the complaints of the Locrians were founded in truth, he should be put to death in prison, and his effects confiscated. That Publius Scipio should be recalled for having quitted his province without the permission of the Senate."

A hot debate followed, in which, " besides the atrocious conduct of Pleminius, much was said about the dress of the general himself, as being not only un-Roman, but even unsoldierly." His critics complained that " he

walked about the gymnasium in a cloak and
slippers, and that he gave his whole time to light
books and the palæstra. That his whole staff
were enjoying the delights which Syracuse
afforded, with the same indolence and effeminacy.
That Carthage and Hannibal had dropped out
of his memory "—somewhat inconsistent on the
part of the people who were proposing to recall
him because he had been fighting with Hannibal.
How petty, but how true to human nature !
The real grievance of his crusted seniors was not
his leniency with Pleminius, but his Greek
refinement and studies.

But wiser counsels prevailed. Metellus pointed
out how inconsistent it would be for the State
now to recall, condemned in his absence and
without a hearing, the very man whom they
had commissioned to finish the war, and to do
so in the face of the Locrians' evidence that
none of their tribulations occurred while Scipio
was there. On the motion of Metellus a commission of inquiry was appointed to visit Scipio
in Sicily, or even in Africa had he departed
thither, with power to deprive him of his command if they found that the acts at Locri had
been committed at his command or with his
concurrence. This commission was also to investigate the charges brought against his military
régime, whether his own alleged indolency or

the relaxation of discipline among the troops. These charges were brought by Cato, who, besides being an adherent of Fabius, conceived it his special mission in life to oppose the new Hellenic culture and to effect cheese-paring economies. It is related that to save money he sold his slaves as soon as they were too old for work, that he esteemed his wife no more than his slaves, and that he left behind in Spain his faithful charger rather than incur the charge of transporting it to Italy. As quæstor under Scipio in Sicily he reproached his general with his liberality to the troops, until Scipio dispensed with his services, whereupon Cato returned disgruntled to Italy to join Fabius in an anti-waste campaign in the Senate.

The commission went first to Locri. Pleminius had already been thrown into prison at Rhegium, according to some accounts by Scipio, who had sent a *legatus* with a guard to seize him and his principal coadjutors. At Locri restitution of their property and civic privileges was made to the citizens, and they willingly agreed to send deputies to give evidence against Pleminius at Rome. But though invited to bring complaints against Scipio, the citizens declined, saying that they were convinced that the injuries inflicted on them were neither by his orders nor with his approval.

The commission, relieved of the duty of investigating such charges, nevertheless went on to Syracuse, to see for themselves the military condition of his command. There are parallels in history to such a political investigation on the eve of a great military venture—the Nivelle affair is the most recent,—and often they have reacted disastrously both on the confidence of the commander and the confidence of his subordinates in him. But Scipio survived the test. "While they were on their way to Syracuse, Scipio prepared to clear himself, not by words but by facts. He ordered all his troops to assemble there, and the fleet to be got in readiness, as though a battle had to be fought that day with the Carthaginians by sea and land. On the day of their arrival he entertained them hospitably, and on the next day presented to their view his land and sea forces, not only drawn up in order, but the former carrying out field operations, while the fleet fought a mock naval battle in the harbour. The prætor and the deputies were then conducted round to view the armouries, the granaries, and other preparations for the war. And so great was the admiration aroused in them of each particular, and the whole together, that they formed the conviction that under the conduct of that general, and with that army, the Carthaginians would be vanquished, or by

none other. They bid him with the blessing
of the gods, cross over. . . . " (Livy).

These deputies were not, as the "frocks"
of 1914-18, remarkable only for their ignorance
of matters military. Like most Romans they
were men of military training and experience,
and no "eye-wash" would have deceived them.
In face of such a verdict it is surprising that a
historian of the reputation of Mommsen should
here again swallow Fabius's spiteful charges,
and repeat as his own the opinion that Scipio
failed to maintain discipline. Only a lay historian,
militarily ignorant, could imagine that an army
which had been allowed to run to seed could
carry out the complex Roman battle drill and
develop its preparations to a pitch of efficiency
that not only gained the approval but aroused
the enthusiasm of this expert commission.

On their return to Rome the warmth of their
praise induced the Senate to vote that Scipio
should cross to Africa, and that he should be
given permission to select himself, *out of those
forces which were in Sicily*, the troops which he
wanted to accompany him. The irony of this
grudging and tardy permission lies in the clause
in italics. He was given their blessing, and
that was all. For a venture of such magnitude,
he was worse supported by the Senate than even
Hannibal by Carthage. Of Roman troops, apart

from his own volunteers, he had in Sicily only
the 5th and 6th Legions, the remnant of those
who had fought at Cannæ, and who in punishment for the defeat had been sentenced to serve
in exile in Sicily. A less understanding commander might well have hesitated to rely on troops
suffering such a degradation. But "Scipio was
very far from feeling contempt for such soldiers,
inasmuch as he knew that the defeat at Cannæ
was not attributable to their cowardice, and
that there were no soldiers in the Roman army
who had served so long, or were so experienced
in the various types of combat." They on
their side were burning to wipe off the unjust
stigma of disgrace, and when he declared that
he would take them with him he could feel
sure that by this proof of his trust and generosity
he had won their utter devotion. He inspected
them "man by man," and putting aside those
unfit for service he filled up their places with
his own men, bringing the strength of each
Legion up to 6200 infantry and 300 horse.

Roman accounts differ widely as to the total
strength of the force that embarked, and even
in Livy's time the uncertainty was such that he
preferred not to give an opinion. The smallest
estimate is 10,000 foot and 200 horse ; a second
is 16,000 infantry and 1600 horse ; the third,
and largest, is a total of 35,000, including horse

and foot. The first is disproved by the previous facts, and these seem rather to point to the second as the correct estimate. In any case it was slender indeed for the object aimed at.

There is a striking parallel between the situation and numbers of Scipio in 204 B.C. and those of Gustavus Adolphus in 1630 A.D., when the Swedish King crossed the Baltic to strike at the seat of the Imperial power. And each force, small as it was, had been welded by the training genius and personal magnetism of its leader into a superb instrument of war—a cadre or frame-work for later expansion. How purely this expedition and its triumphant success was the plan and the work of Scipio can be aptly shown by quoting Mommsen, a far from friendly wit-ness : " It was evident that the Senate did not appoint the expedition, but merely allowed it : Scipio did not obtain half the resources which had formerly been placed at the command of Regulus, and he got that very corps which for years had been subjected by the Senate to intentional degradation. The African army was, in the view of the majority of the Senate, a forlorn hope of disrated companies and vol-unteers, whose loss in any event the State had no great occasion to regret." And yet many historians assert that Rome's victory in the Punic War was due to the generous support

she gave to her generals, the failure of Carthage
to the reverse cause !

Not only were Scipio's means slender, but the
African situation had changed for the worse
during the year's delay forced on him by the
need to raise and train his expeditionary force,
in default of Rome's aid, a delay still further
protracted by the Locri inquiry. Hasdrubal,
son of Gisco, on his return from Spain had check-
mated Scipio's newly won influence over Syphax,
by giving the king his daughter Sophonisba in
marriage, and in return got Syphax to renew his
pledge of alliance with Carthage. Still afraid
that Syphax would adhere to his old pledges to
Scipio, Hasdrubal "took advantage of the Numidian while under the influence of the first
transports of love, and calling to his aid the
caresses of the bride, prevailed upon him to send
envoys into Sicily to Scipio, and by them to warn
him 'not to cross over into Africa in reliance
on his former promise.' " The message begged
Scipio to carry on the war elsewhere, so that
Syphax might maintain his neutrality, adding
that if the Romans came he would be compelled to fight against them.

Passion had beaten diplomacy. One can imagine what a blow the message proved to Scipio.
Yet he determined to carry through his plan,
and merely sought to counteract the moral

harm which might accrue if Syphax's defection
became known.   He sent the envoys back as
quickly as possible, with a stern reminder to
Syphax of his treaty obligations.   Further, realising that the envoys had been seen by many, and
that if he maintained silence about their visit
rumours would spread, Scipio announced to the
troops that the envoys had come, like Masinissa
earlier to Lælius, to urge him to hasten his invasion of Africa.   It was a shrewd ruse, for the
truth might have caused grave moral depression
at the critical time.   Scipio, wiser than the
military authorities of 1914, understood crowd
psychology, and knew that the led put the
worst construction on the silence of the leaders,
that they assume no news to be bad news,
despite all the proverbs.

CHAPTER IX.

AFRICA.

THUS in the spring of 204 B.C. Scipio embarked
his army at Lilybæum (modern Marsala), and
sailed for Africa. His fleet is said to have com-
prised forty warships and four hundred transports, and on board was carried water and rations
for fifty-five days, of which fifteen days' supply
was cooked. Complete dispositions were made
for the protection of the convoy by the warships,
and each class of vessel was distinguished by
lights at night—the transports one, the warships
two, and his own flagship three. It is worth
notice that he personally supervised the embarkation of the troops.

A huge crowd gathered to witness the departure, not only the inhabitants of Lilybæum, but
all the deputies from Sicily—as a compliment
to Scipio,—and the troops who were being left
behind. At daybreak Scipio delivered a fare-
well oration and prayer, and then by a trumpet
gave the signal to weigh anchor. Favoured by

a strong wind the fleet made a quick passage, and next morning when the sun rose they were in sight of land, and could discern the promontory of Mercury (now Cape Bon). Scipio ordered the pilot to make for a landing farther west, but a dense fog coming on later forced the fleet to cast anchor. Next morning, the wind rising, dispelled the fog, and the army disembarked at the Fair promontory (now Cape Farina), a few miles from the important city of Utica. The security of the landing was at once ensured by entrenching a camp on the nearest rising ground.

These two promontories formed the horns, pointing towards Sicily, of the territory of Carthage, that bull's head of land projecting into the Mediterranean which is to-day known as Tunisia. The horns, some thirty-five miles apart, enclosed a vast semicircular bay in the centre of which stood Carthage, on a small peninsula pointing east. Utica lay just below and inside the tip of the western horn, and a few miles east of the city was the Bagradas river, whose rich and fertile valley was the main source of supplies for Carthage. Another strategic point was Tunis, at the junction of the Carthage peninsula with the mainland—geographically south-west of Carthage but militarily east, because it lay across the landward approaches from that flank.

Although the Carthaginians had long been

expecting the blow, and had watch-towers on
every cape, the news created feverish excitement
and alarm, stimulated by the stream of fugitives
from the country districts. At Carthage, emergency defensive measures were taken as if Scipio
was already at the gates. The Roman's first step
was clearly to gain a secure base of operations,
and with this aim his preliminary move was
against Utica. His fleet was despatched there
forthwith while the army marched overland, his
advanced guard cavalry encountering a body
of five hundred Carthaginian horse who had been
sent to reconnoitre and interrupt the landing.
After a sharp engagement these were put to
flight. A still better omen was the arrival of
Masinissa, true to his word, to join Scipio. Livy
states that the earlier sources from which he
compiled his history differed as to the strength
of Masinissa's reinforcement, some saying that
he brought two hundred horse, and some two
thousand. Livy accepts the smaller estimate,
for the very sound reason that Masinissa after
his return from Spain had been driven out of
his father's kingdom by the joint efforts of
Syphax and the Carthaginians, and for the past
year and more had been eluding pursuit by
repeated changes of quarter. An exile, who
had escaped from the last battle with only
sixty horsemen, it is unlikely that he could

have raised his band of followers to any large proportions.

Meanwhile, the Carthaginians despatched a further body of four thousand horse, mainly Numidians, to oppose Scipio's advance and gain time for Syphax and Hasdrubal to come to their aid. To their ally and to their chief general in Africa the most urgent messages had been sent. Hanno with the four thousand cavalry occupied a town, Salæca, about fifteen miles from the Roman camp near Utica, and it is said by Livy that Scipio, on hearing of this, remarked, " What, cavalry lodging in houses during the summer ! Let there be even more in number while they have such a leader." " Concluding that the more dilatory they were in their operations, the more active he ought to be, he sent Masinissa forward with the cavalry, directing him to ride up to the gates of the enemy and draw them out to battle, and when their whole force had poured out and committed themselves thoroughly to the attack, then to retire by degrees." Scipio himself waited for what he judged sufficient time for Masinissa's advanced party to draw out the enemy, and then followed with the Roman cavalry, " proceeding without being seen, under cover of some rising ground." He took up a position near the so-called Tower of Agathocles, on the northern slope of a saddle between two ridges.

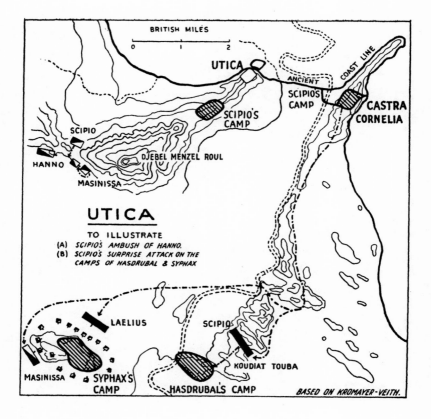

BRITISH MILES

0   1   2

UTICA

ANCIENT

SCIPIO'S
CAMP

COAST LINE

SCIPIO'S
CAMP

CASTRA
CORNELIA

SCIPIO

HANNO

DJEBEL MENZEL ROUL

MASINISSA

UTICA

TO ILLUSTRATE

(A) *SCIPIO'S AMBUSH OF HANNO.*
(B) *SCIPIO'S SURPRISE ATTACK ON THE*
    CAMPS OF HASDRUBAL & SYPHAX

LAELIUS

SCIPIO

MASINISSA

SYPHAX'S
CAMP

KOUDIAT TOUBA

HASDRUBAL'S CAMP

BASED ON KROMAYER-VEITH.

Masinissa, following Scipio's plan, made repeated advances and retirements. At first he drew out small skirmishing parties, then counterattacked them so that Hanno was forced to reinforce them, lured them on again by a simulated retreat and repeated the process. At last Hanno, irritated by these tactical tricks—so typical of the Parthians and the Mongols later,—sallied forth with his main body, whereupon Masinissa retired slowly, drawing the Carthaginians along the southern side of the ridges and past the saddle which concealed the Roman cavalry. When the moment was ripe, Scipio's cavalry emerged and encircled the flank and rear of Hanno's cavalry, while Masinissa, turning about, attacked them in front. The first line of a thousand were surrounded and slain, and of the remainder two thousand were captured or killed in a vigorous pursuit.

Scipio followed up this success by a seven days' circuit through the countryside, clearing it of cattle and supplies, and creating a wide devastated zone as a barrier against attack. Security, both in supply and protection, thus effected, he concentrated his efforts on the siege of Utica, which he wanted for his base of operations. Utica, however, was not destined to be a second Cartagena. Although he combined attack from the sea by the marines with the land assault, the fortress defied all his efforts and ruses.

Hasdrubal by this time had collected a force of thirty thousand foot and three thousand horse, but with painful recollections of the maulings he had suffered in Spain, did not venture to move to Utica's relief until reinforced by Syphax. When the latter at last came, with an army stated to have been fifty thousand foot and ten thousand horse, the menace compelled Scipio to raise the siege—after forty days. Faced with such a concentration of hostile force, Scipio's situation must have been hazardous, but he extricated himself without mishap and fortified a camp for the winter on a small peninsula, connected to the mainland by a narrow isthmus. This lay on the eastern, or Carthage, side of Utica, thus lying on the flank of any relieving force, and was later known as Castra Cornelia. The enemy then encamped some seven miles farther east, covering the approaches to the River Bagradas.

If there is a parallel between Scipio's landing in Africa and Gustavus's landing in Germany, there is a still more striking parallel between their action during the first season on hostile soil. Both campaigns to the unmilitary critic appear limited in scope compared with the avowed object with which they had set forth. Both generals have been criticised for over-caution, if not hesitation. And both were justified not only by the result, but by the science of war. Scipio and Gustavus alike, unable for reasons' outside their control to adjust the means to the end, displayed that rare strategical quality—of adjusting the end to the means. Their strategy foreshadowed Napoleon's maxim that " the whole art of war consists in a well ordered and prudent defensive, followed by a bold and rapid offensive." Both sought first to lay the foundations for the offensive which followed by gaining a secure base of operations where they could build up their means to a strength adequate to ensure the attainment of the end.

Gustavus is known to have been a great student of the classics : was his strategy in 1630 perhaps a conscious application of Scipio's method ? Nor is this campaign of Gustavus's the only military parallel with Scipio's that history records. For the action of Wellington in fortifying and retiring behind the lines of Torres Vedras in 1810 to checkmate the French superior concentration of force has a vivid reminder, both topographical and strategical, of Scipio's action in face of the concentration of Syphax and Hasdrubal.

In this secure retreat Scipio devoted the winter to build up his strength and supplies for the

next spring's campaign. Besides the corn he
had collected in his preliminary foraging march,
he obtained a vast quantity from Sardinia, and
also fresh stores of clothing and arms from
Sicily. The success of his landing, his sharp
punishment of the Carthaginian attempts to
meet him in battle, and, above all, the fact that
he had dissipated the terrors of the unknown,
had falsified all the fears of the wiseacres, by
holding his own, small though his force, on the
dreaded soil of Africa, almost at the gates of
Carthage—all these factors combined to turn the
current of opinion and arouse the State to give
him adequate support. Reliefs were sent to
Sicily so that he could reinforce his strength
with the troops at first left behind for local
defence.

But, as usual, while seeking to develop his
own strength, he did not overlook the value of
subtracting from the enemy's. He reopened
negotiations with Syphax, " whose passion for
his bride he thought might now perhaps have
become satiated from unlimited enjoyment."
In these he was disappointed, for while Syphax
went so far as to suggest terms of peace by
which the Carthaginians should quit Italy in
return for a Roman evacuation of Africa, he
did not hold out any hope that he would abandon
the Carthaginian cause if the war continued.

For such terms Scipio had no use, but he only
rejected them in a qualified manner, in order to
maintain a pretext for his emissaries to visit the
hostile camp. The reason was that he had
conceived a plan whereby to weaken the enemy
and anticipate the attack that he feared owing
to the enemy's heavy superiority of numbers.
Some of his earlier messengers to Syphax had
reported that the Carthaginians' winter huts
were built almost entirely of wood, and those of
the Numidians of interwoven reeds and matting,
disposed without order or proper intervals, and
that a number even lay outside the ramparts
of the camps. This news suggested to Scipio
the idea of setting fire to the enemy's camp and
striking a surprise blow in the confusion.

Therefore in his later embassies Scipio sent
certain expert scouts and picked centurions
dressed as officers' servants. While the confer-
ences were in progress, these rambled through
the camps, both that of Syphax and of Hasdrubal, noting their approaches and entrances
and studying the general plan of the camps, the
distance between them, the times and methods
of stationing guards and outposts. With each
embassy, too, a different lot of observers were
sent, so that as large a number as possible should
familiarise themselves with the lie of the enemy
camps. As a result of their reports Scipio ascer-

tained that Syphax's camp was the more in-
flammable and the easier to attack.

He then sent further envoys to Syphax, who
was hoping for peace, with instructions not to
return until they received a decisive answer on
the proposed terms, saying that it was time
that either an agreement was settled or the war
vigorously prosecuted.   After consultation between Syphax and Hasdrubal, they apparently
decided to accept, whereupon Scipio made further
stipulations, as a suitable way of terminating
the truce, which he did next day, informing
Syphax that while he himself desired peace,
the rest of his council were opposed to it.   By
this means he gained freedom to carry out his
plan without breaking his faith, though he undoubtedly went as close to the border between
strategical ruse and deliberate craft as was possible without overstepping it.

Syphax, much vexed at this breakdown of
negotiations, at once conferred with Hasdrubal,
and it was decided to take the offensive and
challenge Scipio to battle, on level ground if
possible.   But Scipio was ready to strike, his
preparations complete.   Even in his final preparations, he sought to mystify and mislead the
enemy in order to make his surprise more effective.
The orders issued to the troops spoke of the
surprise being aimed at Utica ; he launched his

ships and mounted on board siege machines as if he was about to assault Utica from the sea, and he despatched two thousand infantry to seize a hill which commanded the town. This move had a dual purpose—to convince the enemy that his plan was directed against Utica, and to occupy the city garrison to prevent them making a sortie against his camp when he marched out to attack the hostile camps. Thus he was able to achieve economy of force, by concentrating the bulk of his troops for the decisive blow, and leaving only a slight force to guard the camp, and thus once more he did not lose sight of the principle of security in carrying out that of surprise. He had fixed the enemy's attention in the wrong direction.

About mid-day he summoned a conference of his ablest and most trusted tribunes and disclosed his plan. To this conference he summoned the officers who had been to the enemy's camp. " He questioned them closely and compared the accounts they gave of the approaches and entrances of the camp, letting Masinissa decide, and following his advice owing to his personal knowledge of the ground." Then he ordered the tribunes to give the troops their evening meal early, and lead the legions out of the camp after " Retreat " had been sounded as usual. On this point Polybius adds the interesting note

that " it is the custom among the Romans at
supper-time for the trumpeters to sound their
instruments outside the general's tent as a signal
that it is time to set the night-watches at their
several posts."

About the first watch the troops were formed
up in march order and moved off on their seven-
mile march, and about midnight arrived in the
vicinity of the hostile camps, which were just
over a mile apart. Thereupon Scipio divided his
force, placing all the Numidians and half his
legionaries under Lælius and Masinissa with
orders to attack Syphax's camp. The two commanders he first took aside and urged on them
the need for caution, emphasising that " the more
the darkness in night attacks hinders and im-
pedes the sight, the more must one supply the
place of actual vision by skill and care." He
further instructed them that he would wait to
launch his attack on Hasdrubal's camp until
Lælius had set fire to the other camp, and with
this purpose marched his own men at a slow
pace.

Lælius and Masinissa, dividing their force,
attacked the camp from two directions simultaneously—a convergent manœuvre,—and Masinissa also posted his Numidians, because of their
knowledge of the camp, to cut off the various
exits of escape. As had been foreseen, once the

leading Romans had set the fire alight, it spread rapidly along the first row of huts, and in a brief while the whole camp was aflame, because of the closeness of the huts and the lack of proper intervals between rows.

Fully imagining that it was an accidental conflagration, Syphax's men rushed out of their huts unarmed, and in a disorderly flight. Many perished in their huts while half asleep, many were trampled to death in the frenzied rush for the exits, while those who escaped the flames were cut down unawares by the Numidians posted at the gates of the camp.

Meanwhile in the Carthaginian camp the soldiers, aroused by the sentries' report of the fire in the other camp, and seeing how vast was the volume of flame, rushed out of their own camp to assist in extinguishing the fire, they also imagining it an accident and Scipio seven miles distant. This was as Scipio had hoped and anticipated, and he at once fell on the rabble, giving orders not to let a man escape to give warning to the troops still in the camp. Instantly he followed up this by launching his attack on the gates of the camp, which were unguarded as a result of the confusion.

By the cleverness of his plan in attacking Syphax's camp first, he had turned to advantage the fact that a number of the latter's huts were

outside the ramparts and so easily accessible,
and had created the opportunity to force the
gates of the better protected Carthaginian camp.

The first troops inside set fire to the nearest
huts, and soon the whole camp was aflame, the
same scenes of confusion and destruction being
here repeated, and those who escaped through
the gates meeting their fate at the hands of
Roman parties posted for the purpose. " Hasdrubal at once desisted from any attempt to
extinguish the fire, as he knew now from what
had befallen him that the calamity which had
overtaken the Numidians also was not, as they
had supposed, the result of chance, but was due
to the initiative and daring of the enemy."
He therefore forced his way out and escaped,
along with only two thousand foot and five
hundred horsemen, half-armed and many wounded
or scorched. With this small force he took refuge
in a near-by town, but when Scipio's pursuing
troops came up, and seeing that the inhabitants
were disaffected, he resumed his flight to Carthage. Syphax who had also escaped, probably
with a larger proportion, retired to a fortified
position at Abba, a town quite close.

The armies of Sennacherib had not suffered
a swifter, more unexpected, or more complete
fate than those of Hasdrubal and Syphax.
According to Livy forty thousand men were

either slain or destroyed by the flames, and
about five thousand were captured, including
many Carthaginian nobles. As a spectacle of
disaster it surpasses any in history. Polybius,
who presumably got his information from Lælius
and other eye-witnesses, thus describes it : "The
whole place was filled with wailing and con-
fused cries, panic, fear, strange noises, and
above all raging fire and flames that overbore
all resistance, things any one of which would
be sufficient to strike terror into a human heart,
and how much more this extraordinary combination of them all. It is not possible to find
any other disaster which however magnified
could be compared with this, so much did it
exceed in horror all previous events. Therefore
of all the brilliant exploits performed by Scipio
this seems to me the most brilliant and most
adventurous. . . ."

In Carthage the news caused great alarm and
anxiety—Hasdrubal's purpose in retreating there
had been to allay the panic and forestall any
capitulation. His presence and his resolute
spirit was needed. The Carthaginians had expected with the spring campaign to find their
armies shutting in Scipio on the cape near Utica,
cutting him off by land and sea. Finding the
tables so dramatically turned, they swung from
confidence to extreme despondency. At an

emergency debate in the Senate three different
opinions were put forward: to send envoys to
Scipio to treat for peace; to recall Hannibal;
to raise fresh levies and urge Syphax to renew
the struggle in co-operation with them. The
influence of Hasdrubal, combined with that of
all the Barcine party, carried the day, and the
last policy was adopted. It is worth a passing
note, in view of the charge of ultra-Roman
prejudice often made against Livy, that he
speaks with obvious admiration of this third
motion which " breathed the spirit of Roman
constancy and adversity."

Syphax and his Numidians had at first decided
to continue their retreat and, abandoning the
war, retire to their own country, but three
influences caused them to change their minds.
These were the pleadings of Sophonisba to
Syphax not to desert her father and his people,
the prompt arrival of the envoys from Carthage,
and the arrival of a body of over four thousand
Celtiberian mercenaries from Spain — whose
numbers were exaggerated by popular rumour,
doubtless inspired by the war party, to ten
thousand. Accordingly Syphax gave the envoys
a message that he would co-operate with Hasdrubal, and showed them the first reinforcement
of fresh Numidian levies who had arrived. By
energetic recruiting Hasdrubal and Syphax were

able to take the field again within thirty days, joining forces, and entrenched a camp on the Great Plain. Their strength is put as between thirty and thirty-five thousand fighting men.

Scipio, after his dispersion of the enemy's field forces in the recent surprise, had turned his attention to the siege of Utica, in order to gain the secure base which he wanted as a prelude to further operations. It is evident that he intentionally refrained from pressing the retreat of Syphax, for such pressure by forcing the latter to fight would tend to pour fresh fuel on a fire that was flickering out of itself. The ground for such a hope we have already shown, as also the factors which caused its disappointment. Polybius gives us a valuable sidelight at this juncture on Scipio's care and forethought for his troops—" He also at the same time distributed the booty, but expelled the merchants who were making too good an affair of it; for as their recent success had made them form a rosy picture of the future, the soldiers attached no value to their actual booty, and were very ready to dispose of it for a song to the merchants."

When the news reached Scipio of the junction of the Carthaginian and Numidian forces and of their approach, he acted promptly. Leaving only a small detachment to keep up the appearance of a siege by land and sea, he set out to meet the enemy, his whole force being in light marching order—he evidently judged that rapidity was the key to this fresh menace, to strike before they could weld their new force into a strong weapon. On the fifth day he reached the Great Plain, and fortified a camp on a hill some three and a half miles distant from the enemy's camp. The two following days he advanced his forces, harassing the enemy's outposts, in order to tempt them out to battle. The bait succeeded on the third day, and the enemy's combined army came out of their camp and drew up in order of battle. They placed the Celtiberians, their picked troops, in the centre, the Numidians on the left, and the Carthaginians on the right. " Scipio simply followed the usual Roman practice of placing the maniples of *hastati* in front, behind them the *principes*, and hindmost of all the *triarii*." He disposed his Italian cavalry on his right, facing Syphax's Numidians, and Masinissa's Numidians on his left, facing the Carthaginian horse. At the first encounter the enemy's wings were broken by the Italian and Masinissa's cavalry. Scipio's rapidity of march and foresight in striking before Hasdrubal and Syphax had consolidated their raw levies was abundantly justified. Moreover, on one side moral was heightened by recent success, and on the other lowered by recent disaster.

In the centre the Celtiberians fought staunchly, knowing that flight was useless, because of their ignorance of the country, and that surrender was futile, because of their treason in coming from Spain to take service against the Romans. It would appear that Scipio used his second and third lines—the *principes* and *triarii*—as a mobile reserve to attack the Celtiberians' flanks, instead of to reinforce the *hastati* directly, as was the normal custom. Thus surrounded on all sides the Celtiberians were cut to pieces where they stood, though only after an obstinate resistance, which enabled the commanders, Hasdrubal and Syphax, as well as a good number of the fugitives, to make their escape. Hasdrubal with his Carthaginian survivors found shelter in Carthage, and Syphax with his cavalry retreated home to his own capital, Cirta.

Night had put a stop to the scene of carnage, and next day Scipio sent Masinissa and Lælius in pursuit of Syphax, while he himself cleared the surrounding country, and occupied its strong places, as a preliminary to a move on Carthage. Here fresh alarm had been caused, but the people were more staunch in the hour of trial than is the tendency to regard them. Few voices were raised in favour of peace, and energetic measures were taken for resistance. The city was provisioned for a long siege, and the work of strength-

ening and enlarging the fortifications was pushed
on.   At the same time the Senate decided to
send the fleet to attack the Roman ships
at Utica and attempt to raise the siege, and
as a further step the recall of Hannibal was decided on.

Scipio, lightening his transport by the despatch
of the booty to his camp near Utica, had already
reached and occupied Tunis, with little opposition despite the strength of the place.   Tunis
was only some fifteen miles from Carthage and
could be clearly seen, and as Polybius tells us
of Scipio, " this he thought would be a most
effective means of striking the Carthaginians
with terror and dismay "—the moral objective
again.

Hardly had he completed this " bound," however, before his sentries sighted the Carthaginian
fleet sailing past the place.   He realised what
their plan was and also the danger, knowing
that his own ships, burdened with siege machines
or converted into transports, were unprepared
for a naval battle.   Unhesitatingly, he made
his decision to stave off the threat, and made
a forced march back to Utica.   There was no
time to clear his ships for action, and so he hit
on the plan of anchoring the warships close
inshore, and protecting them by a four-deep row
of transports lashed together as a floating wall.

He also laid planks from one to the other, to
enable the free movement of troops, leaving
narrow intervals for small patrol-boats to pass
in and out under these bridges. He then put
on board the transports a thousand picked men
with a very high proportion of weapons, particularly missiles—an interesting point in fore-
shadowing the modern doctrine of using increased
fire-power in defence to replace man-power.

These emergency measures were completed
before the enemy's attack came, thanks first
to the slow sailing of the Carthaginian fleet,
and their further delay in offering battle in the
open sea. Thus they were forced to sail in
against the Romans' unexpected type of formation, like ships attacking a wall. Their weight
of numbers, too, was partly discounted by the
fact of the transports being higher out of the
water, so that the Carthaginians had to throw
their weapons upwards, and the Romans, con-
versely, gained additional impetus and better
aim through casting their missiles from a superior
height. But the device of sending patrol-boats
and light craft out through the intervals to
harass the Carthaginian ships—a device obviously
adapted by Scipio from military tactics—failed
of its effect, and proved an actual handicap to
the defence. For when they went out to harass
the approaching warships they were run down

by the mere momentum and bulk of the latter,
and in the later stages became so intermingled
with the Carthaginian ships as to mask the fire
of the troops on the transports.

Beaten off in their direct assaults, the Carthaginians tried a new measure, throwing long
beams with iron hooks at the end on to the
Roman transports, these beams being secured
by chains to their own vessels. By this means
the fastenings were broken, and a number of
transports dragged away, the troops manning
them having barely time to leap on to the second
line of ships. Only one line had been broken,
and the opposition had been so severe that the
Carthaginians contented themselves with this
limited success, and sailed back to Carthage.
They towed away six captured transports, though
doubtless more were broken adrift and lost by
the Romans.

Baulked in this quarter, the Carthaginians'
hopes were shattered in another, for the pursuing
force sent by Scipio after Syphax had fulfilled
its object and finally cut away this prop of
Carthaginian power in Africa. The success went
still further, as it gained for Scipio that Numidian source of man-power which he had so
long schemed for, and which he needed to build
up his forces to an adequate strength for his
decisive blow.

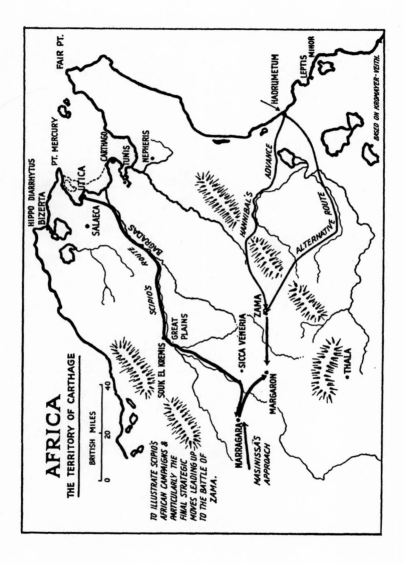

AFRICA
THE TERRITORY OF CARTHAGE

TO ILLUSTRATE SCIPIO'S
AFRICAN CAMPAIGNS &
PARTICULARLY THE
FINAL STRATEGIC
MOVES LEADING UP
TO THE BATTLE OF
ZAMA.

BRITISH MILES

0   20   40

FAIR PT.

PT. MERCURY

HIPPO DIARRHYTUS
BIZERTA

UTICA
SALAECA

CARTHAGO
TUNIS
NEPHERIS

BAGRADAS

SCIPIO'S ROUTE

SOUK EL KREMIS

GREAT
PLAINS

SICCA VENERIA

NARRAGARA

MASINISSA'S
APPROACH

MARGARON

ZAMA

THALA

HANNIBAL'S ADVANCE

ALTERNATIVE ROUTE

HADRUMETUM

LEPTIS
MINOR

BASED ON KROMAYER-VEITH.

Following up Syphax, Lælius and Masinissa arrived in Massylia (Masinissa's hereditary kingdom from which he had been driven) after a fifteen days' march, and there expelled the garrisons left by Syphax. The latter had fallen back farther east to his own dominions, Massæsylia—modern Algeria,—and there, spurred on by his wife, raised a fresh force from the abundant resources of his kingdom. He proceeded to organise them on the Roman model, imagining, like so many military copyists in history, that imitation of externals gave him the secret of the Roman success. His force was large enough—as large, in fact, as his original strength,—but it was utterly raw and undisciplined. With this he advanced to meet Lælius and Masinissa. At the first encounter between the opposing cavalry, numerical superiority told, but the advantage was lost when the Roman infantry reinforced the intervals of their cavalry, and before long the raw troops broke and fled. The victory was essentially one due to superior training and discipline, and not to any subtle manœuvre such as appears in all Scipio's battles. This is worth note in view of the fact that some historians lose no opportunity of hinting that Scipio's success was due more to his able lieutenants than to himself.

Syphax, seeing his force crumbling, sought to

shame his men into resistance by riding forward and exposing himself to danger. In this gallant attempt he was unhorsed, made prisoner, and dragged into the presence of Lælius. As Livy remarks, this was " a spectacle calculated to afford peculiar satisfaction to Masinissa." The latter showed fine military spirit as well as judgment after the battle, when he declared to Lælius that, much as he would like to visit his regained kingdom, " it was not proper in prosperity any more than in adversity to lose time." He therefore asked permission to push on with the cavalry to Cirta, Syphax's capital, while Lælius followed with the infantry. Having won Lælius's assent, Masinissa advanced, taking Syphax with him. On arrival in front of Cirta, he summoned the principal inhabitants to appear, but they refused until he showed them Syphax in chains, whereupon the faint-hearted threw open the gates. Masinissa, posting guards, galloped off to seize the palace, and was met by Sophonisba. This woman, almost as famous as Helen or Cleopatra for her beauty and for her disastrous influence, made such a clever appeal to his pride, his pity, and his passion, that she not only won his pledge not to hand her over to the Romans, but " as the Numidians are an excessively amorous race, he became the slave of his captive." When she had withdrawn, and he had

to face the problem of how to reconcile his duty
with his pledge, his passion suggested to him a
loophole—to marry her himself that very day.
When Lælius came up he was so annoyed that
at first he was on the point of having her dragged
from the marriage-bed and sent with the other
captives to the Utica camp, but afterwards
relented, agreeing to leave the decision to Scipio.
The two then set to work on the reduction of
the remaining towns in Numidia, which were
still garrisoned by the troops of Syphax.

When the captives arrived at Scipio's camp,
Syphax himself in chains at their head, the
troops poured out to see the spectacle. What
a contrast with a few years back ! Now, a
captive in chains ; then, a powerful ruler who
held the balance of power, for whose friendship
Scipio and Hasdrubal vied on their simultaneous
visits, both placing themselves in his power, so
highly did they assess the prize at stake.

This thought evidently passed through Scipio's
mind, the recollection, too, of their quondam
friendship, and moved him to sympathy. He
questioned Syphax as to the motives that had
led him to break his pledge of alliance with the
Romans and make war on them unprovoked.
Syphax, gaining confidence from Scipio's manner,
replied that he had been mad to do so, but
that taking up arms was only the consumma-

tion of his frenzy, and not its beginning, which
dated from his marriage to Sophonisba. "That
fury and pest" had fascinated and blinded him
to his undoing. But ruined and fallen as he was,
he declared that he gained some consolation
from seeing her fatal lures transferred to his
greatest enemy.

These words caused Scipio great anxiety, for
he appreciated both her influence and the menace
to the Roman plans from Masinissa's hasty
wedding. She had detached one passionate
Numidian; she might well lead astray another.
When Lælius and Masinissa arrived shortly after,
Scipio showed no signs of his feelings in his
public greeting, praising both in the highest
terms for their work. But as soon as possible
he took Masinissa aside privately. His talk
with the delinquent was a masterpiece of tact
and psychological appeal. "I suppose, Masinissa, that it was because you saw in me some
good qualities that you first came to me when
in Spain for the purpose of forming a friendship
with me, and that afterwards in Africa you
committed yourself and all your hopes to my
protection. But of all those virtues, which
made me seem worthy of your regard, there is
none of which I am so proud as temperance
and control of my passions." Then pointing
out the dangers caused by want of self-control,

he continued : " I have mentioned with delight,
and I remember with pleasure, the instances of
fortitude and courage you displayed in my
absence. As to other matters, I would rather
that you should reflect on them in private,
than that I should cause you to blush by reciting
them." Then, with a final call to Masinissa's
sense of duty, he dismissed him. Where reproaches might have stiffened Masinissa, such
a friendly appeal broke him down, and bursting
into tears, he retired to his own tent. Here,
after a prolonged inward struggle, he sent for a
confidential servant, and ordered him to mix
some poison in a cup and carry it to Sophonisba,
with the message that " Masinissa would gladly
have fulfilled the first obligation which as a
husband he owed to her, his wife ; but as those
who had the power had deprived him of the
exercise of those rights, he now performed his
second promise—that she should not come alive
into the power of the Romans." When the
servant came to Sophonisba she said, " I accept
this nuptial present ; nor is it an unwelcome
one, if my husband can render me no better
service. Tell him, however, that I should have
died with greater satisfaction had I not married
so near on my death." Then, calmly and without
a quiver, she took and drained the cup.

As soon as Scipio heard the news, fearing that

the high-spirited young man, when so distraught,
might take some desperate step, " he immediately sent for him, and at one time endeavoured
to solace him, at another gently rebuked him
for trying to expiate one rash act with another,
and making the affair more tragical than was
necessary."

Next day Scipio sought to erase this grief from
Masinissa's mind by a well-calculated appeal
to his ambition and pride. Summoning an
assembly, he first saluted Masinissa by the
title of king, speaking in the highest terms of
his achievements, and then presented him with
a golden goblet, an ivory sceptre, a curule chair,
and other symbols of honour. " He increased
the honour by observing that among the Romans
there was nothing more magnificent than a
' triumph,' and that those who received the
reward of a ' triumph ' were not invested with
more splendid ornaments than those of which
the Roman people considered Masinissa alone,
of all foreigners, worthy." This action, and the
encouragement to his dreams of becoming master
of all Numidia, had the desired effect, and
Masinissa speedily forgot his private sorrows in
his public distinction. Lælius, whom Scipio
had been careful to praise similarly and reward,
was then sent with Syphax and the other captives
back to Rome.

CHAPTER X.

A VIOLATED PEACE.

His political base in Africa secured, Scipio
moved back to Tunis, and this time the moral
threat, strengthened by recent events, was successful. It tilted the scales against the war party,
and the Carthaginians sent thirty of their principal elders—the Council of Elders being superior
even to the Senate—to beg for terms of peace.
According to Livy, they prostrated themselves
in Eastern manner on entering Scipio's presence,
and their pleas showed equal humility. They
implored pardon for their State, saying that it
had been twice brought to the brink of ruin
by the rashness of its citizens, and they hoped
it would again owe its safety to the indulgence
of its enemies. This hope was based on their
knowledge that the Roman people's aim was
dominion, and not destruction, and they declared
that they would accept whatever terms he saw
fit to grant. Scipio replied " that he had come
to Africa with the hope, which had been in-

creased by his success, that he should carry
home victory and not terms of peace.   Still,
though he had victory in a manner within his
grasp, he would not refuse accommodation, that all
the nations might know that the Roman people
both undertake and conclude wars with justice."

The terms which he laid down were :   the
restoration of all prisoners and deserters, the withdrawal of the Carthaginian armies from Italy and
Gaul and all the Mediterranean islands, the giving
up of all claim to Spain, the surrender of all their
warships except twenty.   A considerable, but
not heavy, indemnity in grain and money was
also demanded.   He gave them three days'
grace to decide whether to accept these terms,
adding that if they accepted they were to make
a truce with him and send envoys to the Senate
at Rome.

The moderation of these terms is remarkable,
especially considering the completeness of Scipio's
military success.   It is a testimony not only to
Scipio's greatness of soul, but to his transcendent
political vision.   Viewed in conjunction with
his similar moderation after Zama, it is not too
much to say that Scipio had a clear grasp of what
is just dawning on the mind of the world to-day—
that the true national object in war, as in peace,
is a more perfect peace.   War is the result of a
menace to this policy, and is undertaken in order

to remove the menace, and by the subjugation
of the will of the hostile State " to change this
adverse will into a compliance with our own
policy, and the sooner and more cheaply in lives
and in money we can do this, the better chance
is there of a continuance of national prosperity
in the widest sense. The aim of a nation in war
is, therefore, to subdue the enemy's will to
resist with the least possible human and economic
loss to itself." [1] The lesson of history, of very
recent history moreover, enables us to deduce
this axiom, that " A military victory is not in
itself equivalent to success in war." [2] Further,
as regards the peace terms, " the contract must
be reasonable ; for to compel a beaten foe to
agree to terms which cannot be fulfilled is to
sow the seeds of a war which one day will be
declared in order to cancel the contract." [2]
There is only one alternative — annihilation.
Mommsen's comment on Scipio's moderation
over these terms is that they " seemed so singu-
larly favourable to Carthage, that the question
obtrudes itself whether they were offered by
Scipio more in his own interest or in that of
Rome." A self-centred seeker after popularity

[1] 'Paris, or the Future of War,' by Captain B. H. Liddell
Hart. 1925.
[2] 'The Foundations of the Science of War,' by Colonel
J. F. C. Fuller. 1926.

would surely have prolonged the war to end
it with a spectacular military decision, rather
than accept the paler glory of a peace by agreement. But Mommsen's insinuation, as also his
judgment, is contradicted by Scipio's similar
moderation after Zama, despite the extreme
provocation of a broken treaty.

These terms the Carthaginians accepted, and
complied with the first provision by sending
envoys to Scipio to conclude a truce and also
to Rome to ask for peace, the latter taking with
them a few prisoners and deserters, as a diplomatic promissory note. But the war party had
again prevailed, and though ready to accept
the peace negotiations as a cloak and a means
of gaining time, they sent an urgent summons
to Hannibal and Mago to return to Africa. The
latter was not destined to see his homeland,
for wounded just previously in an indecisive
battle, he died of his injuries as his fleet of
transports was passing Sardinia.

Hannibal, anticipating such a recall, had
already prepared ships and withdrawn the main
strength of his army to the port, keeping only
his worst troops as garrisons for the Bruttian
towns. It is said that no exile leaving his own
land ever showed deeper sorrow than Hannibal
on quitting the land of his enemies, and that
he cursed himself that he had not led his troops

on Rome when fresh from the victory of Cannæ.
" Scipio," he said, " who had not looked at a
Carthaginian enemy in Italy, had dared to go
and attack Carthage, while he, after slaying a
hundred thousand men at Trasimene and Cannæ,
had suffered his strength to wear away around
Casilinum, Cannæ, and Nola."

The news of his departure was received in
Rome with mingled joy and apprehension, for
the commanders in southern Italy had been
ordered by the Senate to keep Hannibal in play,
and so fix him while Scipio was securing the decision in Africa. Now, they felt that his presence
in Carthage might rekindle the dying embers of
the war and endanger Scipio, on whose single
army the whole weight of the war would fall.

On the arrival of Lælius in Rome, amid up-
roarious scenes of jubilation, the Senate had
decided that he should remain there until the
Carthaginians' envoys arrived. With the envoys
of Masinissa mutual congratulations were ex-
changed, and the Senate not only confirmed
him in the title of King conferred by Scipio,
but presented him by proxy with further presents
of honour and the military trappings usually
provided for a consul. They also acceded to his
request to release their Numidian captives, a
politic step by which he hoped to strengthen
his hold on his countrymen.

When the envoys from Carthage arrived, they addressed the Senate in terms similar to those they had used to Scipio, putting the whole blame on Hannibal, and arguing that so far as Carthage was concerned the peace which closed the First Punic War remained unbroken. This being so they craved to continue the same peace terms. A debate followed in the Senate, which revealed a wide conflict of opinion, some advocating that no decision should be taken without the advice of Scipio, others that the war should at once be renewed, as Hannibal's departure suggested that the request for peace was a subterfuge. Lælius, called on for his opinion, said that Scipio had grounded his hopes of effecting a peace on the assurance that Hannibal and Mago would not be recalled from Italy. The Senate failed to come to a definite decision, and the debate was adjourned, though it would appear from Polybius that it was renewed later, and a settlement reached.

Meanwhile, however, the war had already restarted in Africa by a violation of the truce. While the embassy was on its way to Rome, fresh reinforcements and stores had been sent from Sardinia and Sicily to Scipio. The former arrived safely, but the convoy of two hundred transports from Sicily encountered a freshening gale when almost within sight of Africa, and though the warships struggled into harbour, the transports were blown towards Carthage; the greater part to the island of Ægimurus— thirty miles distant at the mouth of the Bay of Carthage,—and the rest were driven on to the shore near the city. The sight caused great popular excitement, the people clamouring that such immense booty should not be missed. At a hasty assembly, into which the mob penetrated, it was agreed that Hasdrubal should cross over to Ægimurus with a fleet and seize the transports. After they had been brought in, those that had been driven ashore near Carthage were refloated and brought into harbour.

Directly Scipio heard of this breach of the truce he despatched three envoys to Carthage to take up the question of this incident, and also to inform the Carthaginians that the Roman people had ratified the treaty; for despatches had just arrived for Scipio with this news. The envoys, after a strong speech of protest, delivered the message that while "the Romans would be justified in inflicting punishment, they entreated them in the name of the common fortune of mankind not to push the matter to an issue, but rather let their folly afford a proof of the generosity of the Romans." The envoys then retired for the Senate to debate. Resentment at the bold language of the envoys, reluctance

to give up the ships and their supplies, new
confidence from Hannibal's imminent help, combined to turn the scales against the peace party.
It was decided simply to dismiss the envoys
without a reply. The latter, who had barely
escaped from mob violence on arrival, requested
an escort on their return journey, and two
triremes were assigned them. This fact gave
some of the leaders of the war party an idea
whereby to detonate a fresh explosion which
should make the breach irreparable. They sent
to Hasdrubal, whose fleet was then anchored off
the coast near Utica, to have some ships lying
in wait near the Roman camp to attack and
sink the envoys' ship. Under orders, the commanders of the escort quitted the Roman quinquereme when within sight of the Roman camp.
Before it could make the harbour it was attacked
by three Carthaginian quadriremes despatched
for the purpose. The attempt to board her was
beaten off, but the crew, or rather the survivors,
only saved themselves by running the ship
ashore.

This dastardly action drove Scipio to renew
operations for the final trial of strength. An
immediate move direct on Carthage was impossible, for this would have meant a long siege,
and to settle down to siege operations in face
of the imminent arrival of Hannibal, who might

menace his rear and cut his communications, would have been madness. Nor was his own situation pleasant, for not only had he suffered the heavy loss of the supplies and reinforcements from Sicily, but Masinissa was absent with his own and part of the Roman force—ten cohorts. Immediately on the conclusion of the provisional treaty Masinissa had set out for Numidia to recover his own kingdom, and, with the assistance of the Romans, add that of Syphax to it.

When the truce was broken, Scipio sent urgent and repeated messages to Masinissa, telling him to raise as strong a force as possible and rejoin him with all speed. Then, having taken measures for the security of his fleet, he deputed the command of the Roman base to his legate Bæbius, and started on a march up the valley of the Bagradas, aiming to isolate Carthage, and by cutting off all supplies and reinforcements from the interior undermine its strength as a preliminary to its direct subjugation—the principle of security once more. On his march, he no longer consented to receive the submission of towns which offered to surrender, but took them all by assault, and sold the inhabitants as slaves—to show his anger and impress the moral of the Carthaginians' violation of the treaty.

During this " approach " march—for such it was in fact if not in semblance—the envoys returning from Rome reached the naval camp. Bæbius at once despatched the Roman envoys to Scipio, but detained the Carthaginians, who, hearing of what had befallen, were naturally distressed as to their own fate. But Scipio, to his credit, refused to avenge on them the maltreatment of his own envoys. " For, aware as he was of the value attached by his own nation to keeping faith with ambassadors, he took into consideration not so much the deserts of the Carthaginians as the duty of the Romans. Therefore restraining his own anger and the bitter resentment he felt, he did his best to preserve ' the glorious record of our fathers,' as the saying is." He sent orders to Bæbius to treat the Carthaginian envoys with all courtesy and send them home. " The consequence was that he humiliated all the people of Carthage and Hannibal himself, by thus requiting in ampler measure their baseness by his generosity." (Polybius.)

In this act Scipio revealed his understanding of the ethical object in war, and of its value. Chivalry governed by reason is an asset both in war and in view of its sequel—peace. Sensible chivalry should not be confounded with the quixotism of declining to use a strategical or tactical advantage, of discarding the supreme moral weapon of surprise, of treating war as

if it were a match on the tennis court—such
quixotism as is typified by the burlesque of
Fontenoy, "Gentlemen of France, fire first."
This is merely stupid. So also is the traditional
tendency to regard the use of a new weapon as
"hitting below the belt," regardless of whether
it is inhuman or not in comparison with existing
weapons. So the Germans called the use of
tanks an atrocity, and so did we term gas—so
also the mediæval knight spoke of firearms
when they came to interfere with his safe slaughter
of unarmoured peasants. Yet the proportion of
combatants slain in any battle decreased as
much when firearms superseded the battleaxe
and sword as when gas came to replace shell
and the bullet. This antagonism to new weapons
is mere conservatism, not chivalry.

But chivalry, as in this example of Scipio's,
is both rational and far-sighted, for it endows
the side which shows it with a sense of superiority, and the side which falls short with a sense
of inferiority. The advantage in the moral
sphere reacts on the physical.

If this chivalrous act of Scipio's was partly
the fruit of such psychological calculation, it
was clearly in accord also with his natural
character, for his attitude earlier in Spain shows
that it was no single theatrical gesture. Just
as in war we cannot separate the moral from

the mental or physical spheres, so also in assessing character. We cannot separate the nobility of Scipio's moral conduct, throughout his career, from the transcendent clearness of his mental vision—they blended to form not only a great general but a great man.

Some time before this, probably during the episode which broke the truce, Hannibal had landed at Leptis—in what to-day is the Gulf of Hammamet—with twenty-four thousand men, and had moved to Hadrumetum. Stopping here [1] to refresh his troops, he sent an urgent appeal to the Numidian chief Tychæus, who "was thought to have the best cavalry in Africa," to join him in saving the situation. He sought to play on the fears of Tychæus, who was a relative of Syphax, by the argument that if the Romans won he would risk losing his dominion, and his life too, through Masinissa's greed of power. As a result, Tychæus responded, and came with a body of two thousand horse. This was a welcome accession, for Hannibal had lost his old superiority in cavalry, his master-weapon. In addition Hannibal could expect, and shortly received, the twelve thousand troops

[1] Livy says for a few days only, and Polybius is obscure on the point, but the known factors suggest a longer stay, because of the inevitable time required for the arrival of Tychæus's cavalry, and the junction with him of the other Carthaginian forces.

of Mago's force from Liguria, composed of Gauls who had shown their fine quality in the last battle before the recall; also a large body of new levies raised in Africa, whose quality would be less assuring. Further—according to Livy,— four thousand Macedonians had recently come to the aid of Carthage, sent by King Philip.

Let this force once reach Carthage and be able to base its operations on such a fortress, and source of reinforcement, and the situation would turn strongly in favour of Hannibal. In contrast, Scipio had been robbed of the bulk of his supplies and reinforcements, he was isolated on hostile soil, part of his force was detached with Masinissa, and the strength the latter could recruit was still uncertain.

It is well to weigh these conditions, for they correct common but false historical impressions. At this moment the odds were with Hannibal, and the feeling in the rival capitals, as recorded by Livy and Polybius, is a true reflection of the fact.

CHAPTER XI.

ZAMA.

EVEN at this critical juncture, jealousy of Scipio was rife in the Roman Senate. His backing, as all through, came from the people, not from his military rivals in the Senate. The consuls had done nothing to assist Scipio's campaign through fixing Hannibal in Italy, save that Servilius advanced to the shore after Hannibal was safely away. But at the beginning of the year when the allocation of the various provinces was decided, according to custom, both consuls pressed for the province of Africa, eager to reap the fruits of Scipio's success and thus earn glory cheaply. Metellus again tried to play the part of protecting deity. As a result the consuls were ordered to make application to the tribunes for the question to be put to the people to decide whom they wished to conduct the war in Africa. All the tribes thereupon nominated Scipio. Despite this emphatic popular verdict, the consuls drew lots for the province of Africa, having persuaded the Senate to make a decree to this effect. The lot fell to Tiberius Claudius, who was given an equal command with Scipio, and an armada of fifty quinqueremes for his expedition. Happily for Scipio, this jealousy-inspired move failed to prevent him putting the coping-stone on his own work, for Claudius was slow over his preparations, and when he eventually set out was caught in a storm and driven to Sardinia. Thus he never reached Africa.

Soon, too, as news of the changed situation in Africa filtered through, Scipio's detractors combined with the habitual pessimists in the distillation of gloom. They recalled that " Quintus Fabius, recently deceased, who had foretold how arduous the contest would be, had been accustomed to predict that Hannibal would prove a more formidable enemy in his own country than he had been in a foreign one ; and that Scipio would have to encounter not Syphax, a king of undisciplined barbarians . . . ; nor his father-in-law Hasdrubal, that most fugacious general " —a Fabian libel on a man of undaunted spirit ; " nor tumultuary armies hastily collected out of a crowd of half-armed rustics, but Hannibal . . . who, having grown old in victory, had filled Spain, Gaul, and Italy with monuments of his vast achievements ; who commanded troops of equal length of service ; troops hardened

by superhuman endurance ; stained a thousand
times with Roman blood. . . ." The tension in
Rome was increased by the past years of indecisive warfare, carried on languidly and apparently endless, whereas now Scipio and Hannibal
had stimulated the minds of all as generals
prepared for a final death-clinch.

In Carthage the scales of public opinion
appear to have been evenly balanced, on the one
hand gaining confidence from Hannibal's achievements and invincibility, on the other depressed
by reflection on Scipio's repeated victories, and
on the fact that through his sole efforts they had
lost their hold on Spain and Italy—as if he had
been " a general marked out by destiny, and
born, for their destruction."

On the threshold of this final phase, the
support, moral and material, given to Hannibal
by his country seems to have been, on balance,
more than that accorded to Scipio—one more
nail in the coffin of a common historical error.

His situation, already discussed, was one to
test the moral fibre of a commander. Security
lies often in calculated audacity, and an analysis
of the military problems makes it highly probable
that his march inland up the Bagradas valley
was aimed, by its menace to the rich interior on
which Carthage depended for supplies, to force
Hannibal to push west to meet him instead of

north to Carthage. By this clever move he
threatened the economic base of Carthage and
protected his own, also luring Hannibal away
from his military base—Carthage.

A complementary purpose was that this line
of movement brought him progressively nearer
to Numidia, shortening the distance which Masinissa would have to traverse with his expected
reinforcement of strength. The more one studies
and reflects on this manœuvre, the more masterly
does it appear as a subtly blended fulfilment
of the principles of war.

It had the intended effect, for the Carthaginians sent urgent appeals to Hannibal to
advance towards Scipio and bring him to battle,
and although Hannibal replied that he would
judge his own time, within a few days he marched
west from Hadrumetum, and arrived by forced
marches at Zama. He then sent out scouts to
discover the Roman camp and its dispositions
for defence—it lay some miles farther west.
Three of the scouts, or spies, were captured,
and when they were brought before Scipio he
adopted a highly novel method of treatment.
" Scipio was so far from punishing them, as is
the usual practice, that on the contrary he
ordered a tribune to attend them and point out
clearly to them the exact arrangement of the
camp. After this had been done he asked them

if the officer had explained everything to their
satisfaction. When they answered that he had
done so, Scipio furnished them with provisions
and an escort, and told them to report carefully
to Hannibal what had happened to them "
(Polybius). This superb insolence of Scipio's
was a shrewd blow at the moral objective,
calculated to impress on Hannibal and his troops
the utter confidence of the Romans, and corre-
spondingly give rise to doubts among themselves.
This effect must have been still further increased
by the arrival next day of Masinissa with six
thousand foot and four thousand horse. Livy
makes their arrival coincide with the visit of the
Carthaginian spies, and remarks that Hannibal
received this information, like the rest, with no
feelings of joy.

The sequel to this incident of the scouts has
a human interest of an unusual kind. " On
their return, Hannibal was so much struck with
admiration of Scipio's magnanimity and daring,
that he conceived . . . a strong desire to meet
him and converse with him. Having decided
on this he sent a herald saying that he desired
to discuss the whole situation with him, and
Scipio, on receiving the herald's message, accepted
and said that he would send to Hannibal, fixing
a place and hour for the interview. He then
broke up his camp and moved to a fresh site

not far from the town of Narragara, his position
being well chosen tactically, and having water
" within a javelin's throw." He then sent to
Hannibal a message that he was now ready for
the meeting. Hannibal also moved his camp
forward to meet him, occupying a hill safe and
convenient in every respect except that he was
rather too far away from water, and his men
suffered considerable hardship as a result. It
looks as if Scipio had scored the first trick in
the battle of wits between the rival captains!
The second trick also, because he ensured a battle
in the open plain, where his advantage in cavalry
could gain its full value. He was ready to trump
Hannibal's master-card.

On the following day both generals came out
of their camps with a small armed escort, and then,
leaving these behind at an equal distance, met
each other alone, except that each was attended
by one interpreter. Livy prefaces the account
of the interview with the remark that here met
" the greatest generals not only of their own
times, but of any to be found in the records
of preceding ages . . ."—a verdict with which
many students of military history will be inclined to agree, and even to extend the scope
of the judgment another two thousand years.

Hannibal first saluted Scipio and opened the
conversation. The accounts of his speech, as

of Scipio's, must be regarded as only giving its
general sense, and for this reason as also the
slight divergences between the different authorities may best be paraphrased, except for some
of the more striking phrases.   Hannibal's main
point was the uncertainty of fortune—which,
after so often having victory almost within his
reach, now found him coming voluntarily to
sue for peace.   How strange, too, the coincidence
that it should have been Scipio's father whom
he met in his first battle, and now he came to
solicit peace from the son!   "Would that neither
the Romans had ever coveted possessions outside
Italy, nor the Carthaginians outside Africa,
for both had suffered grievously."   However, the
past could not be mended, the future remained.
Rome had seen the arms of an enemy at her
very gates ; now the turn of Carthage had come.
Could they not come to terms, rather than
fight it out to the bitter end ?   "I myself am
ready to do so, as I have learnt by actual experience how fickle Fortune is, and how by a
slight turn of the scale either way she brings
about changes of the greatest moment, as if
she were sporting with little children.   But I
fear that you, Publius, both because you are
very young, and because success has constantly
attended you both in Spain and in Africa, and you
have never up to now at least fallen into the

counter-current of Fortune, will not be convinced by my words, however worthy of credit
they may be." Let Scipio take warning by
Hannibal's own example. "What I was at
Trasimene and at Cannæ, that you are this day."
"And now here am I in Africa on the point of
negotiating with you, a Roman, for the safety
of myself and my country. Consider this, I
beg you, and be not over-proud." ". . . What
man of sense, I ask, would rush into such danger
as confronts you now?" The chance of a single
hour might blot out all that Scipio had achieved
—let him remember the fate of Regulus, from
whom likewise the Carthaginians had sought
peace on African soil. Hannibal then outlined
his peace proposals—that Sicily, Sardinia, and
Spain should be definitely given up to Rome,
and Carthage confine her ambitions to Africa.
In conclusion he said that if Scipio felt a natural
doubt as to the sincerity of the proposals, after
his recent experience, he should remember that
these came from Hannibal himself, the real
power, who would guarantee so to exert himself
that no one should regret the peace. Hannibal
later was to prove both his sincerity and the
truth of this guarantee. But in the circumstances of the moment and of the past, Scipio
had good ground for doubt.

To Hannibal's overture he pointed out that it

was easy to express regret that the two powers
had gone to war—but who had begun it ? Had
Hannibal even proposed them before the Romans
crossed to Africa, and voluntarily retired from
Italy, his proposals would almost certainly have
been accepted. Yet in spite of the utterly
changed position, with the Romans " in command
of the open country," Hannibal now proposed
easier terms than Carthage had already accepted
in the broken treaty. All he offered, in fact, was
to give up territory which was already in Roman
possession, and had been for a long time. It
was futile for him to submit such empty concessions to Rome. If Hannibal would agree
to the conditions of the original treaty, and
add compensation for the seizure of the transports during the truce, and for the violence
offered to the envoys, then he would have something to lay before his council. Otherwise,
" the question must be decided by arms." This
brief speech is a gem of clear and logical reason-
ing. Hannibal apparently made no advance on
his former proposals, and the conference therefore
came to an end, the rival commanders returning
to their camps.

Both sides recognised the issues that hung
upon the morrow—" the Carthaginians fighting
for their own safety and the dominion of Africa,
and the Romans for the empire of the world.

Is there any one who can remain unmoved in
reading the narrative of such an encounter ?
For it would be impossible to find more valiant
soldiers, or generals who had been more successful and were more thoroughly experienced in
the art of war, nor indeed had Fortune ever
offered to contending armies a more splendid
prize of victory " (Polybius). If the prize was
great, so was the price of defeat. For the
Romans if beaten were isolated in the interior
of a foreign land, while the collapse of Carthage
must follow if the army that formed her last
bulwark was beaten. These crucial factors were
stressed by the opposing commanders when next
morning at daybreak they led out their troops
for the supreme trial, and had made their
dispositions.

Scipio rode along the lines and addressed his
men in a few appropriate words. Polybius's
account, though necessarily but the substance
and not an exact record, is so in tune with
Scipio's character as to be worth giving. " Bear
in mind your past battles and fight like brave
men worthy of yourselves and of your country.
Keep it before your eyes that if you overcome
your enemies not only will you be unquestioned
masters of Africa, but you will gain for yourselves
and your country the undisputed command and
sovereignty of the rest of the world. But if

the result of the battle be otherwise, those who have fallen bravely in the fight will be for ever shrouded in the glory of dying thus for their country, while those who save themselves by flight will spend the remainder of their lives in misery and disgrace. For no place in Africa will afford you safety, and if you fall into the hands of the Carthaginians it is plain enough to those who reflect what fate awaits you. May none of you, I pray, live to experience that fate, now that Fortune offers us the most glorious of prizes ; how utterly craven, nay, how foolish shall we be, if we reject the greatest of goods and choose the greatest of evils from mere love of life. Go, therefore, to meet the foe with two objects before you, either victory or death. For men animated by such a spirit must always overcome their adversaries, since they go into battle ready to throw their lives away." Of this address Livy says " he delivered these remarks with a body so erect, and with a countenance so full of exultation, that one would have supposed that he had already conquered."

On the other side Hannibal ordered each commander of the foreign mercenaries to address his own men, appealing to their greed for booty, and bidding them be sure of victory from his presence and that of the forces he had brought back. With the Carthaginian levies he ordered

their commanders to dwell on the sufferings of
their wives and children should the Romans
conquer. Then to his own men he spoke personally, reminding them of their seventeen years'
comradeship and invincibility, of the victory of
Trebia won over the father of the present Roman
general, of Trasimene and Cannæ—" battles with
which the action in which we are about to
engage is not worthy of comparison." Speaking
thus, he bade them cast their eyes on the opposing army and see for themselves that the Romans
were fewer in numbers, and further, only a frac-
tion of the forces they had conquered in Italy.

The dispositions made by the rival leaders
have several features of note. Scipio placed
his heavy Roman foot—he had probably two
legions—in the centre ; Lælius with the Italian
cavalry on the left wing, and on the right wing
Masinissa with the whole of the Numidians,
horse and foot, the latter presumably prolonging
the centre and the cavalry on their outer flank.

The heavy infantry were drawn up in the
normal three lines, first the *hastati*, then the
principes, and finally the *triarii*. But instead
of adopting the usual chequer formation, with
the maniples of the second line opposite to and
covering the intervals between the maniples of
the first line, he ranged the maniples forming
the rear lines directly behind the respective

maniples of the first line. Thus he formed wide
lanes between each cohort—which was primarily
composed of one maniple of *hastati*, one of *principes*, and one of *triarii*.

His object was twofold : on the one hand, to
provide an antidote to the menace of Hannibal's
war elephants and to guard against the danger
that their onset might throw his ranks into
disorder; on the other, to oil the working of his
own machine by facilitating the sallies and
retirements of his skirmishers. These *velites*
he placed in the intervals in the first line, ordering
them to open the action, and if they were forced
back by the charge of the elephants, to retire.
Even this withdrawal he governed by special
instructions, ordering those who had time to
fall back by the straight passages and pass
right to the rear of the army, and those who were
overtaken to turn right or left as soon as they
passed the first line, and make their way along
the lateral lanes between the lines. This wise
provision economised life, ensured smooth func-
tioning, and increased the offensive power—a
true fulfilment of economy of force. It may
even be termed the origin of modern extended
order, for its object was the same—to nega-
tive the effect of the enemy's projectiles by
creating empty intervals, a reduction of the
target by dispersion, the only difference being

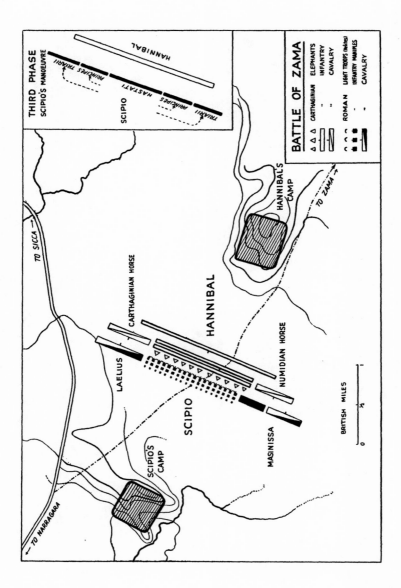

THIRD PHASE
SCIPIO'S MANOEUVRE

HANNIBAL

PRINCIPES TRIARII

SCIPIO

PRINCIPES HASTATI

TRIARII

BATTLE OF ZAMA

CARTHAGINIAN   ELEPHANTS
                INFANTRY
                CAVALRY

ROMAN   LIGHT TROOPS (velites)
                INFANTRY MANIPLES
                CAVALRY

TO SICCA

TO NARRAGARA

LAELIUS

CARTHAGINIAN HORSE

SCIPIO

SCIPIO'S CAMP

MASINISSA

HANNIBAL

NUMIDIAN HORSE

HANNIBALS CAMP

TO ZAMA

BRITISH MILES

0   ¼   ½

that Hannibal's projectiles were animal, not mineral.

The Carthaginian had eighty elephants, more than in any previous battle, and in order to terrify the enemy he placed them in front of his line. Supporting them, in the first line, were the Ligurian and Gallic mercenaries intermixed with Balearic and Moorish light troops. These were the troops with whom Mago had sailed home, about twelve thousand in number, and it is a common historical mistake to regard the whole force as composed of light troops.

In the second line Hannibal placed the Carthaginian and African levies as well as the Macedonian force, their combined strength probably exceeding that of the first line. Finally Hannibal's own troops formed the third line, held back more than two hundred yards distant from the others, in order evidently to keep it as an intact reserve, and lessen the risk of it becoming entangled in the mêlée before the commander intended. On the wings Hannibal disposed his cavalry, the Numidian allies on the left and the Carthaginian horse on the right. His total force was probably in excess of fifty thousand, perhaps fifty-five thousand. The Roman strength is less certain, but if we assume that each of Scipio's two legions was duplicated by an equal body of Italian allies, and add Masi-

nissa's ten thousand, the complete strength
would be about thirty-six thousand if the legions
were at full strength. It was probably less,
because some wastage must have occurred during
the earlier operations since quitting his base.

The First Phase.—The battle opened, after
preliminary skirmishing between the Numidian
horse, with Hannibal's orders to the drivers
of the elephants to charge the Roman line.
Scipio promptly trumped his opponent's ace,
by a tremendous blare of trumpets and cornets
along the whole line. The strident clamour so
startled and terrified the elephants that many
of them at once turned tail and rushed back
on their own troops. This was especially the
case on the left wing, where they threw the
Numidians, Hannibal's best cavalry wing, into
disorder just as they were advancing to the
attack. Masinissa seized this golden opportunity
to launch a counter-stroke, which inevitably
overthrew the disorganised opponents. With
Masinissa in hot pursuit, they were driven from
the field, and so left the Carthaginian left wing
exposed.

The remainder of the elephants wrought much
havoc among Scipio's *velites*, caught by their
charge in front of the Roman line. But the foresight that had provided the " lanes " and laid
down the method of withdrawal was justified by

its results. For the elephants took the line of least resistance, penetrating into the lanes rather than face the firm-knit ranks of the heavy infantry maniples. Once in these lanes the *velites* who had retired into the lateral passages, between the lines, bombarded them with darts from both sides. Their reception was far too warm for them to linger when the door of escape was held wide open. While some of the elephants rushed right through, harmlessly, and out to the open in rear of the Roman army, others were driven back out of the lanes and fled towards the Carthaginian right wing. Here the Roman cavalry received them with a shower of javelins, while the Carthaginian cavalry could not follow suit, so that the elephants naturally trended towards the least unpleasant side. " It was at this moment that Lælius, availing himself of the disturbance created by the elephants, charged the Carthaginian cavalry and forced them to headlong flight. He pressed the pursuit closely, as likewise did Masinissa." Both Hannibal's flanks were thus stripped bare. The decisive manœuvre of Cannæ was repeated, but reversed.

Scipio was certainly an artist in tactical " boomerangs," as at Ilipa so now at Zama his foresight and art turned the enemy's best weapon back upon themselves. How decisive might have been the charge of the elephants is shown by the havoc they wrought at the outset among the *velites*.

The Second Phase.—In the meantime the infantry of both armies had "slowly and in imposing array advanced on each other," except that Hannibal kept his own troops back in their original position. Raising the Roman war-cry on one side, polyglot shouts on the other—this vocal discord was a moral drawback,—the lines met. At first the Gauls and Ligurians had the balance of advantage, through their personal skill in skirmishing and more rapid movement. But the Roman line remained unbroken, and the weight of their compact formation pushed the enemy back despite losses. Another factor told, for while the leading Romans were encouraged by the shouts from the rear lines, coming on to back them up, Hannibal's second line—the Carthaginians—failed to support the Gauls, but hung back in order to keep their ranks firm. Forced steadily back, and feeling they had been left in the lurch by their own side, the Gauls turned about and fled. When they tried to seek shelter in the second line, they were repulsed by the Carthaginians, who, with apparently sound yet perhaps unwise military instinct, deemed it essential to avoid any disarray which might enable the Romans to penetrate their line. Exasperated and now

demoralised, many of the Gauls tried to force
an opening in the Carthaginian ranks, but the
latter showed that their courage was not deficient
and drove them off. In a short time the relics
of the first line had dispersed completely, or
disappeared round the flanks of the second line.
The latter confirmed their fighting quality by
thrusting back the Roman first line—the *hastati*
—also. In this they were helped by a human
obstacle, the ground encumbered with corpses
and slippery with blood, which disordered the
ranks of the attacking Romans. Even the
principes had begun to waver when they saw
the first line driven back so decisively, but their
officers rallied them and led them forward in
the nick of time to restore the situation. This
reinforcement was decisive. Hemmed in, because
the Roman formation produced a longer frontage
and so overlapped the Carthaginian line, the
latter was steadily cut to pieces. The survivors
fled back on the relatively distant third line,
but Hannibal continued his policy of refusing
to allow the fugitives to mix with and disturb
an ordered line. He ordered the foremost ranks
of his " Old Guard " to lower their spears as a
barrier against them, and they were forced to
retreat towards the flanks and the open ground
beyond.

The Third Phase.—The curtain now rose on

what was practically a fresh battle. The Romans " had penetrated to their real antagonists, men equal to them in the nature of their arms, in their experience of war, in the fame of their achievements. . . ." Livy's tribute is borne out by the fierceness and the for long uncertain issue of the subsequent conflict, which gives the lie to those who pretend that Hannibal's " Old Guard " was but a shadow of its former power in the days of Trasimene and Cannæ.

The Romans had the moral advantage of having routed two successive lines, as well as the cavalry and elephants, but they had now to face a compact and fresh body of twenty-four thousand veterans, under the direct inspiration of Hannibal. And no man in history has shown a more dynamic personality in infusing his own determination in his troops.

The Romans, too, had at last a numerical advantage, not large, however—Polybius says that the forces were "nearly equal in numbers," —and in reality still less than it appeared. For, while all Hannibal's third line were fresh, on Scipio's side only the *triarii* had not been engaged, and these represented but half the strength of the *hastati* or *principes*. Further, the *velites* had been so badly mauled that they had to be relegated to the reserve, and the cavalry were off the field, engaged in the pursuit.

Thus it is improbable that Scipio had at his
disposal for this final blow more than eighteen
or twenty thousand infantry, less the casualties
these had already suffered.

His next step is characteristic of the man—
of his cool calculation even in the heart of a battle
crisis. Confronted by this gigantic human wall—
such the Carthaginians would appear in phalanx,
—he sounds the recall to his leading troops,
and it is a testimony to their discipline that
they respond like a well-trained pack of hounds.
Then in face of an enemy hardly more than a
bow-shot distant he not only reorganises his
troops but reconstructs his dispositions! His
problem was this—against the first two enemy
lines the Roman formation, shallower than the
Carthaginian phalanx and with intervals, had
occupied a wider frontage and so enabled him
to overlap theirs. Now, against a body double
the strength, his frontage was no longer, and
perhaps less than Hannibal's. His appreciation
evidently took in this factor, and with it two
others. First, that in order to concentrate his
missile shock power for the final effort it would
be wise to make his line as solid as possible,
and this could be done because there was no
longer need or advantage for retaining intervals
between the maniples. Second, that as his
cavalry would be returning any moment, there

was no advantage in keeping the orthodox formation in depth and using the *principes* and *triarii* as a direct support and reinforcement to his front line. The blow should be as concentrated as possible in time and as wide as possible in striking force, rather than a series of efforts. We see him, therefore, making his *hastati* close up to form a compact centre without intervals. Then similarly he closes each half of his *principes* and *triarii* outwards, and advances them to extend the flank on either wing. The order from right to left of his now continuous line would thus be half the *triarii*, half the *principes*, the *hastati*, the other half of the *principes*, the other half of the *triarii*. He now once more overlaps the hostile front. To British readers this novel formation of Scipio's, inspired by a flash of genius in the middle of a momentous conflict, should have a special interest. For here is born the " line " which the Peninsular War and Waterloo have made immortal, here Scipio anticipated Wellington by two thousand years in revealing the truth that the long shallow line is the formation which allows of the greatest volume of fire, which fulfils the law of economy of force by bringing into play the fire—whether bullets or javelins—of the greatest possible proportion of the force. The rôle of Scipio's infantry in the final phase was to fix Hannibal's force

ready for the decisive manœuvre to be delivered
by the cavalry. For this rôle violence and
wideness of onslaught was more important than
sustenance. Scipio made his redistribution de-
liberately and unhurriedly—the longer he could
delay the final tussle the more time he gained for
the return of his cavalry. It is not unlikely
that Masinissa and Lælius pressed the pursuit
rather too far, and so caused an unnecessary
strain on the Roman infantry and on Scipio's
plan. For Polybius tells us that when the rival
infantries met " the contest was for long doubtful,
the men falling where they stood out of determination, until Masinissa and Lælius arrived
providentially at the proper moment." Their
charge, in the enemy's rear, clinched the decision,
and though most of Hannibal's men fought
grimly to the end, they were cut down in their
ranks. Of those who took to flight few escaped,
nor did the earlier fugitives fare any better,
for Scipio's cavalry swept the whole plain, and
because of the wide expanse of level country,
found no obstacle to their searching pursuit.

Polybius and Livy agree in putting the loss
of the Carthaginians and their allies at twenty
thousand slain and almost as many captured.
On the other side, Polybius says that " more
than fifteen hundred Romans fell," and Livy,
that " of the victors as many as two thousand

fell." The discrepancy is explained by the word
" Romans," for Livy's total clearly includes the
allied troops. It is a common idea among
historians that these figures are an underestimate,
and that in ancient battles the tallies given
always minimise the losses of the victor. Ardant
du Picq, a profound and experienced thinker,
has shown the fallacy of these cloistered historians. Even in battle to-day the defeated side
suffers its heaviest loss after the issue is decided,
in what is practically the massacre of unresisting
or disorganised men. How much more must
this disproportion have occurred when bullets,
still less machine-guns, did not exist to take
their initial toll of the victors. So long as forma-
tions remained unbroken the loss of life was
relatively small, but when they were isolated or
dissolved the massacre began.

" Hannibal, slipping off during the confusion
with a few horsemen, came to Hadrumetum,
not quitting the field till he had tried every
expedient both in the battle and before the
engagement ; having, according to the admission
of Scipio, acquired the fame of having handled
his troops on that day with singular judgment "
(Livy). Polybius's tribute is equally ungrudging :
" For, firstly, he had by his conference with
Scipio attempted to end the dispute by himself
alone ; showing thus that while conscious of

his former successes he mistrusted Fortune, and
was fully aware of the part that the unexpected
plays in war. ' In the next place, when he offered
battle, he so managed matters that it was impossible for any commander to make better
dispositions for a contest against the Romans
than Hannibal did on that occasion. The order
of a Roman force in battle makes it very difficult
to break through, for without any change it
enables every man individually and in common
with his fellows to present a front in any direction,
the maniples which are nearest to the danger
turning themselves by a single movement to face
it. Their arms also give the men both protection and confidence, owing to the size of the
shield and owing to the sword being strong
enough to endure repeated blows. . . . But
nevertheless to meet each of these assets Hannibal
had shown supreme skill in adopting . . . all
such measures as were in his power and could
reasonably be expected to succeed. For he had
hastily collected that large number of elephants,
and had placed them in front on the day of the
battle in order to throw the enemy into confusion and break his ranks. He had placed the
mercenaries in advance with the Carthaginians
behind them, in order that the Romans before
the final engagement might be fatigued by their
exertions, and that their swords might lose their

edge . . . and also in order to compel the
Carthaginians thus hemmed in front and rear to
stand fast and fight, in the words of Homer :
' That e'en the unwilling might be forced to
fight.'

"The most efficient and steadfast of his troops
he had held in rear at an unusual distance in
order that, anticipating and observing from afar
the course of the battle, they might with un-
diminished strength and spirit influence the
battle at the right moment. If he, who had never
yet suffered defeat, after taking every possible
step to ensure victory, yet failed to do so, we
must pardon him. For there are times when
Fortune counteracts the plans of valiant men,
and again at times, as the proverb says, ' A
brave man meets another braver still,' as we
may say happened in the case of Hannibal."

Using this proverb in the sense that Polybius
clearly meant it, here in a brief phrase is our
verdict on the battle—a master of war had met
a greater master. Hannibal had no Flaminius
or Varro to face. No longer was a complacent
target offered him by a Roman general, conservative and ignorant of the "sublime part of
war" like those who first met Hannibal in
Italy, unwilling recipients of his instructional
course. At Zama he faced a man whose vision
had told him that in a cavalry superiority lay

the master-card of battle ; whose diplomatic genius had led him long since to convert, in spirit and in effect, Hannibal's source of cavalry to his own use ; whose strategic skill had lured the enemy to a battle-ground where this newly gained power could have full scope and offset his own numerical weakness in the other arms.

Rarely has any commander so ably illustrated the meaning of that hackneyed phrase " gaining and retaining the initiative." From the day when Scipio had defied the opinion of Fabius, monument of orthodoxy, and moved on Carthage instead of on the " main armed forces of the enemy," [1] he had kept the enemy dancing to his tune. Master in the mental sphere, he had compassed their moral disintegration to pave the way for the final act—their overthrow in the physical sphere. That this followed is less remarkable than the manner of its execution. Scipio is almost unique in that as a tactician he was as consummate an artist as in his strategy. Of few of the great captains can it be said that their tactical rivalled their strategical skill, or the reverse. Napoleon is an illustration. But in battle as in the wider field Scipio achieved

---

[1] Two thousand years later this is still the unshakable dogma of orthodox military opinion, despite the hard lessons of 1914-18, when the armies battered out their brains against the enemy's strongest bulwark.

that balance and blend of the mental, moral, and physical sphere which distinguishes him in the roll of history. Thus it came about that on the battlefield of Zama Scipio not only proved capable of countering each of Hannibal's points, but turned the latter's own weapon back upon himself to his mortal injury. Scan the records of time and we cannot find another decisive battle where two great generals gave of their best. Arbela, Cannæ, Pharsalus, Breitenfeld, Blenheim, Leuthen, Austerlitz, Jena, Waterloo, Sedan—all were marred by fumbling or ignorance on one side or the other.

CHAPTER XII.

AFTER ZAMA.

THE completeness of the victory left no room
for a strategic pursuit, but Scipio did not linger
in developing the moral exploitation of his victory. " Concluding that he ought to bring
before Carthage everything which could increase
the consternation already existing there . . . he
ordered Gneius Octavius to conduct the legions
thither by land; and setting out himself from
Utica with the fresh fleet of Lentulus added
to his former one, made for the harbour of
Carthage " (Livy). The immediate move achieved
its object, a bloodless capitulation, thus crown-
ing his eight years' fulfilment of the law of
economy of force by saving the costly necessity
of a siege.

A short distance from the harbour of Carthage
he was met by a ship decked with fillets and
branches of olive. " There were ten deputies,
the leading men in the State, sent at the instance
of Hannibal to solicit peace, to whom, when they

had come up to the stern of the general's ship,
holding out the badges of suppliants and en-
treating the protection and compassion of Scipio,
the only answer given was that they must come
to Tunis, whither he would move his camp.
After taking a view of Carthage, not with any
particular object of acquainting himself of it,
but to dispirit the enemy, he returned to Tunis,
and also recalled Octavius there " (Livy).   The
army on its way had received word that Ver-
mina, the son of Syphax, was on his way to the
succour of Carthage with a large force.   But
Octavius, employing a part of the infantry and
all the cavalry, intercepted their march and
routed them with heavy loss, his cavalry block-
ing all the routes of escape.

As soon as the camp at Tunis was pitched,
thirty envoys arrived from Carthage, and to
play on their fears they were kept waiting a
day without an answer.   At the renewed audience
next day Scipio began by stating briefly that
the Romans had no call to treat them with
leniency, in view not only of their admission
that they had begun the war, but of their recent
treachery in violating a written agreement they
had sworn to observe.

" But for our own sake and in consideration
of the fortune of war and of the common ties of
humanity we have decided to be clement and

magnanimous. This will be evident to you also, if you estimate the situation rightly. For you should not regard it as strange if we impose hard obligations on you or if we demand sacrifices of you, but rather it should surprise you if we grant you any favours, since Fortune owing to your own misconduct has deprived you of any right to pity or pardon, and placed you at the mercy of your enemies." Then he stated first the indulgences, and next the conditions of peace —from that day onward the Romans would abstain from devastation or plunder; the Carthaginians were to retain their own laws and customs, and to receive no garrison; Carthage was to be restored all the territory in Africa that had been hers before the war, to keep all her flocks, herds, slaves, and other property. The conditions were—that reparation was to be made to the Romans for the injuries inflicted during the truce; the transports and cargoes then seized were to be given up; all prisoners and deserters were to be handed over. The Carthaginians were to surrender all their warships except ten triremes, all their elephants, and not to tame any more—Scipio evidently held these in more respect than some modern military historians do. The Carthaginians were not to make war at all on any nation outside Africa, and on no nation in Africa without consulting

Rome. They were to restore to Masinissa, within boundaries that should subsequently be settled, all the territory and property that had belonged to him or his forbears. They were to furnish the Roman army with sufficient corn for three months, and pay the troops until the peace mission had returned from Rome. They were to pay an indemnity of ten thousand talents of silver, in equal annual instalments spread over fifty years. Finally, they were to give as surety a hundred hostages, to be chosen by Scipio from their young men between fourteen and thirty years. The restoration of the transports was to be an immediate condition of a truce, "otherwise they would have no truce, nor any hope of peace."

202 B.C.—1919 A.D. ! What moderation compared with the conditions of Versailles. Here was true grand strategy—the object a better peace, a peace of security and prosperity. Here were sown no seeds of revenge. The necessary guarantees of security were obtained by the surrender of the Carthaginian fleet, by the hostages, and by placing a strong and loyal watchdog in Masinissa next door to Carthage. But they were kept down to the minimum both of cost to the conqueror and hardship to the conquered. This cheaply afforded security paved the way for the future prosperity of Rome, and

at the same time made possible, justly, the revival of Carthage's prosperity.

The vindication of Scipio's generous and foresighted moderation lies in the fifty years of
peace, unspotted on the Carthaginian side, which
followed Zama. And had the Roman politicians
been as wise and dispassionate as Scipio this
peace would of a certainty have endured, with
Carthage a prosperous and placid satellite of
Rome, and the immortal phrase, *Delenda est
Carthago,* instead of being translated into dread-
ful fact, would have been no more than the
transitory hobby-horse of a senile " die-hard,"
a jest for a generation and then forgotten. Moreover, had the execution of the treaty terms been
left with Scipio, there would not have been that
malignant distortion of its clauses whereby constant complaints, but no more, were wrung
from a long-suffering State. Even as it was,
despite these constant petty inflictions, Carthage
became as prosperous and populous as in the
height of its power, and only by deliberate and
outrageous provocation—the order to the citizens
to destroy their own city—could these patient
traders be forced into the revolt that afforded
the desired pretext for their obliteration.

Let it be added that the moderation of Scipio
called forth the response of Hannibal, and the
true peace initiated by the former was being

faithfully fulfilled by the latter, until the un-
relenting hatred of the Roman Senate drove him
into exile from the country whose peaceful prosperity he was rebuilding. Not for the last time
in history, the vision and humanity of two great
rival soldiers gave a shining example of true
policy to revengeful and narrow-minded politicians. Yet for this constructive wisdom Hannibal paid by exile and forced suicide, Scipio
by ending his days in voluntary exile from a
State that had long since " dropped the pilot."
His envious and narrow political rivals in the
Senate could not refuse to ratify his peace terms
in face of his influence over the people, and
were for the moment too conscious of relief in
this happy ending of a ruinous and prolonged
struggle. But as the memory of danger passed,
and also of how narrowly they had escaped, these
checks on their hatred waned, and they could
not forgive " the man who had disdained to
punish more thoroughly the crime of having
made Romans tremble."

When Scipio had announced the terms of peace
to the envoys from Carthage, they carried them
at once to their Senate. His moderation did
not evoke an instant echo in an assembly that
was coincidently " indisposed for peace and unfit
for war." One of the Senators was about to
oppose the acceptance of the terms, and had

begun his speech when Hannibal came forward
and pulled him down from the tribune. The
other members became irate at this breach of
senatorial usage, whereupon Hannibal rose again,
and, admitting that he had been hasty, asked
their pardon for this " unparliamentary " conduct, saying, that as they knew, he had left
at nine years of age, and returned after thirty-
six years' absence on more practical debating.
He asked them to dwell rather on his patriotism,
for it was due to this that he had offended against
senatorial usage. " It seems to me astounding
and quite incomprehensible, that any man who
is a citizen of Carthage, and is conscious of the
designs that we all individually and as a body
have entertained against Rome, does not bless
his stars that now he is at the mercy of the
Romans he has obtained such lenient terms. If
you had been asked but a few days ago what you
expected your country to suffer in the event of
a Roman victory, you would not have been able
even to voice your fears, so extreme were the
calamities then in prospect. So now I beg you
not to argue the question, but to agree unanimously to the terms, and to pray, all of you,
that the Roman people may ratify the treaty." [1]

[1] While this is a Roman version of Hannibal's speech, the
comments ascribed to him are justified by the peace terms, and
it is unlikely that the Romans would give him undue credit for
a pacific influence.

This dust-dispelling breeze of common-sense so cleared their minds that they voted to accept the terms, and the Senate at once sent envoys with instructions to agree to them.

They had some difficulty in complying with the preliminary conditions for the truce, as although they could find the transports they could not return their cargoes, because much of the property was still in the hands of the irreconcilables. The envoys were forced to ask Scipio to accept a monetary compensation, and as he put no obstacles in the way, a three months' truce was settled and granted.

The envoys sent to Rome were chosen from the first men in the State—for the Romans had made it a ground of complaint that the former embassy lacked age and authority,—and they were further recommended to the Roman Senate by the inclusion of Hasdrubal Hædus, a consistent peace advocate and longstanding opponent of the Barcine party. This good impression he, as spokesman, developed by a speech that subtly flattered their dispassionate justice, and while tactfully admitting guilt, toned down its blackness.

The majority of the Senate were clearly in favour of peace, but Lentulus, who had succeeded to Claudius's consulship and also his ambition for cheap glory, protested against the deci-

sion of the Senate, as he had been canvassing
to be allotted Africa as his province, and hoped
that if he could keep alive the dying embers of
the war he might attain his ambition. But this
was promptly snuffed out, for when the question
was put to the assembly of the people, they
unanimously voted that the Senate should make
peace, that Scipio should be empowered to grant
it, and that he alone should conduct the army
home. The Senate therefore agreed accordingly,
and on the return of the Carthaginian envoys
peace was concluded on the terms set forth by
Scipio. The terms were punctually fulfilled, and
Scipio ordered the warships, five hundred in
number, to be towed out to the open sea and
there set on fire—the funeral pyre of Carthaginian
supremacy.

Scipio's enemies used in later years to insinuate
that the moderation of his terms was due to his
fear that harsher conditions might, by prolonging the war, force him to share his glory with a
successor. As this vulgar motive has also been
hinted at by some historians, it is worth while
to stress two facts which utterly demolish the
slander. First, the helplessness and passivity
of Carthage from that time onward; second,
the way the Roman people squashed all attempts
to supersede him during this last phase. After
Zama, when all Rome was wild with enthusiasm,

no usurper, however pushful, would have stood
the least chance of success.

Before leaving Africa, he first saw Masinissa
established in his kingdom, and presented him
with the lands of Syphax, delaying his own
triumph in order to ensure the reward of his
loyal assistants.   Then at last, his task accomplished, he withdrew his army of occupation,
and embarked them for Sicily.   On arriving there
he sent the bulk of his troops on by sea while
he proceeded overland through Italy, one long
triumphal procession, for not only did the people
of every town turn out to do him honour, but
the country folk thronged the roads.   On arriving in Rome he " entered the city in a ' triumph '
of unparalleled splendour, and afterwards distributed to each of his soldiers four hundred
asses out of the spoils."   At this time, too, was
born his surname of Africanus, " the first general
who was distinguished by a name derived from
the country which he had conquered."   Whether
this was bestowed by his soldiers, by his friends,
or as a popular nickname is uncertain.

The enthusiasm of the people was so great
that he could have obtained a title far more
definite than any nickname, however distinguished.   We know from a speech of Tiberius
Gracchus, years later in the darkest hour of
Scipio's career, that the people clamoured to

make him perpetual consul and dictator, and
that he severely rebuked them for striving to
exalt him to what would have been, in reality
if not in name, regal power. The authenticity
of the fact is the more assured because Gracchus
was then charging him with disregarding the
authority of the tribunes. From this speech we
also learn that Scipio " hindered statues being
erected to him in the comitium, in the rostrum,
in the Senate house, in the Capitol, in the chapel
of Jupiter's temple, and that he prevented a
decree being passed that his image, in a triumphal habit, should be brought in procession out
of the temple of Jupiter. . . . Such particulars
as these, which even an enemy acknowledged
while censuring him . . . would demonstrate an
uncommon greatness of mind, in limiting his
honours conformably with his position as a
citizen " (Livy).

Is there any other man in all history who has
put aside so great a prize when it was not only
within his reach but pressed upon him ? The
incident of Cincinnatus returning to his farm
after accomplishing his mission as dictator is
immortal, yet Scipio's not only paralleled but
eclipsed it. Which was the greater test—for a
simple tribesman to conform to the traditions of
a primitive State, or for a highly cultured and
ambitious man of the world to eschew the virtual

kingship of a supreme civilised power ? Compare, again, Scipio's action with the picture of Cæsar reluctantly refusing, in face of the groans of the multitude, the royal diadem which was offered by pre-arrangement with his supporters. In assessing the world's great figures, other than the definitely religious, we have tended to base our estimate mainly on concrete achievement and mental calibre, overlooking the moral values —the same lack of balance between the three spheres which has been remarked in the conduct of policy in peace and war. Even this test of achievement has been based on quantity rather than quality. That Cæsar's work is known universally, and Scipio little more than a name to the ordinary educated man, is a curious reflection on our historical standards, for the one inaugurated the world dominion of Roman civilisation, the other paved the way for its decay.

Extraordinary as is the nobility of mind which led Scipio to this self-abnegation, it becomes yet more so in view of his age. It is conceivable that a man in the last lap of life might have gained a philosophical outlook on the prizes of ambition, and spurned them from experience of their meretricious glitter. But that a man who at the early age of thirty-five had scaled the Himalayan peaks of achievement and fame should do so is a miracle of human nature. Little wonder that his countrymen gradually turned from adulation to petty criticism; little wonder that historians have forgotten him, for such loftiness of mind is beyond the comprehension of ordinary men— and ordinary men hate what they cannot understand.

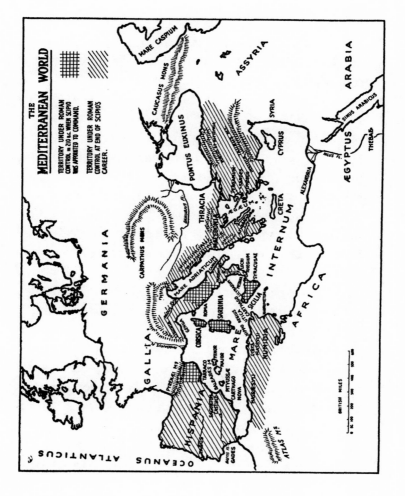

CHAPTER XIII.

SIESTA.

AFTER being for eight of the most critical years
of Rome's life the central figure, Scipio, for the
remainder of his life, comes only at intervals
into the limelight of history. He had saved
Rome physically, and now by retiring into
private citizenship he sought to save her morally.
If a man who had attained such unapproachable
heights of fame could sink his own ambition
and interests, and show that the State was
greater than the individual, the example might
influence later generations. Supreme self-sacri-
fice has been one of the greatest moral forces in
the civilisation of the world. But the force of
Scipio's example was unhappily to be submerged
by the self-seeking of such men as Marius, Sulla,
and Cæsar.

To trace the latter and longer part of his career
is difficult—the curtain is raised only on a series
of brief scenes. We hear of him concerned with
the resettlement of his soldiers ; to each of his

Spanish and African veterans is allotted land in the proportion of two acres for every year's active service. Then three years after Zama he was elected censor, an office which was not only one of the higher magistracies, but regarded as the crown of a political career. As the title implies, the censors, two in number, conducted the census, which was not merely a registration but an occasion for checking the condition of public and private life. It was then that the censors issued edicts concerning the moral rules they intended to enforce, then that they punished irregularities of conduct, and then that they chose fresh members of the Senate. The censors were immune from responsibility for their acts, and the only limitation was that re-election was forbidden, and that no act was valid without the assent of both censors. Scipio's period of office seems to have been marked by unusual harmony, and a clean sheet as regards punishments.

We have to wait until 192 B.C. before we hear of him again, and once more the incident is an illuminating example of his generosity and breadth of view. In the seven years since the peace after Zama, Hannibal had been turning his genius into new channels—the restoration of Carthage's prosperity and the improvement of its administration. But in this labour he incurred the hostility

of many of his own countrymen.   In his efforts
to safeguard the liberty of the people he stopped
the abuse of the judicial power—an abuse which
recalls the worst days of Venice.   Similarly,
finding that the revenue could not raise the
annual payment to Rome without fresh taxation,
he made an investigation into the embezzlement
which lay at the root of this faulty administration.   Those who had been plundering the public
combined with the order of judges to instigate the
Romans against Hannibal.   The Romans, whose
fear of the great Carthaginian had not faded, had
been watching with envy and distrust the commercial revival of Carthage.   They eagerly seized
on such a pretext for intervention.   From Livy,
however, we learn that " a strenuous opposition
was for long made to this by Scipio Africanus,
who thought it highly unbecoming the dignity
of the Roman people to make themselves a party
to the animosities and charges against Hannibal ;
to interpose the public authority in the faction
strife of the Carthaginians, not deeming it sufficient to have conquered that commander in the
field, but to become as it were his prosecutors
in a judicial process. . . ."   Scipio's opposition
delayed but it could not stop the lust for revenge
of smaller men—Cato was consul,—and an embassy was sent to Carthage to arraign Hannibal.
He, realising the futility of standing his trial,

decided to escape before it was too late, and sailed for Tyre, lamenting the misfortunes of his country oftener than his own.

At the beginning of the next year Scipio was elected consul for the second time, and his election along with Tiberius Longus afforded a coincidence in that their fathers had been consuls together in the first year of the Hannibalic war. Scipio's second consulship was comparatively uneventful, at least in a military sense, for the Senate decided that as there was no immediate foreign danger both consuls should remain in Italy. To this decision Scipio was strongly opposed, though he bowed to it, and once again history was to confirm his foresight and rebuke the " wait and see " policy of the near-sighted Roman Senators.

During the interval between Zama and his second consulship, Rome had been engaged in a struggle in Greece. The freedom of action which Zama conferred had combined with certain earlier factors to re-orient, or more literally to orient, her foreign policy. Ever since the repulse of Pyrrhus, Rome had been driving towards an inevitable contact with the Near East. Here the three great powers were the empires into which after Alexander the Great's death his vast dominion had been divided—Macedon, Egypt, and Syria, or, as it was then termed, Asia.

With Egypt, Rome had made an alliance eighty years before, and this alliance had been cemented by commercial ties. But Philip V. of Macedon had allied himself with Hannibal, and though his help was verbal rather than practical, the threat of an attack on Italy had driven the Romans to take the offensive against him, with the aid of a coalition of the Greek States. The drain on her resources elsewhere made Rome seize the first chance, in 205 B.C., for an indecisive peace. Taking advantage of her preoccupation with Hannibal, Philip made a compact with Antiochus of Syria to seize on and share the dominions of Egypt.

But after Zama, Rome was free to respond to the appeal of her ally, and eager also to take revenge for Philip's unneutral act in sending four thousand Macedonians to aid Hannibal in the final battle. The Senate, however, could only persuade the assembly of the people—anxious to enjoy the fruits of peace—by pretending that Philip was on the point of invading Italy. At Cynoscephalæ the legion conquered the phalanx, and Philip was forced to accept terms which reduced him to a second-rate power—like Carthage, stripped of his foreign possessions, and forbidden to make war without the consent of Rome.

The Roman Senate did not realise, however,

that this removal of the Macedonian danger
made war inevitable with Antiochus of Syria,
for the tide of Roman dominion clearly threatened his own submersion sooner or later. Rome
had in effect swallowed first Carthage and then
Macedon, and Antiochus had no liking for the
rôle of Jonah. The Mediterranean world was too
small to hold them both. Antiochus, inflated
with his own grandiloquent title of "King of
Kings," decided to take the initiative and en-
large his own dominions while the opportunity
was good. In 197-196 B.C. he overran the whole
of Asia Minor, and even crossed into Thrace.

Greece was obviously his next objective, but
the Romans could not see this, though Scipio
did. In a prophetic speech he declared "that
there was every reason to apprehend a dangerous
war with Antiochus, for he had already, of his
own accord, come into Europe ; and how did
they suppose he would act in future, when he
should be encouraged to a war, on one hand
by the Ætolians, avowed enemies of Rome, and
stimulated, on the other, by Hannibal, a general
famous for his victories over the Romans ? "—for
Hannibal had recently moved to the court of
Antiochus. But the Senate, acting like the pro-
verbial ostrich, rejected this advice, and decided
that not only should no new army be sent to
Macedonia, but that the one which was there

should be brought home and disbanded. Had Scipio been allotted Macedonia as his province, the danger from Antiochus might have been nipped in the bud and the subsequent invasion of Greece prevented.

Politically, the main feature of his year of office was a wide extension of the policy of settling colonies of Roman citizens throughout Italy—a safeguard against such a dangerous revolt of the Italian States as had followed the invasion of Hannibal. Scipio himself enjoyed the honour of being nominated by the censors as prince of the Senate, an office which apart from its honour had greater influence than that of president, which it had replaced. For the president's functions were limited to those of the modern "Speaker," whereas the prince of the Senate could express his opinions as well as presiding.

The only serious hostilities during this year were in north-western Italy, where the Insubrian and Ligurian Gauls and the Boii had made one of their periodical risings. Longus, the other consul, whose province it was, moved against the Boii. Finding how strong and determined were their forces, he sent post-haste to Scipio, asking him, if he thought proper, to join him. The Gauls, however, seeing the consul's defensive attitude and guessing the reason, attacked at

once before Scipio could arrive. It is evident
that the Romans narrowly escaped a disaster,
but the battle was sufficiently indecisive for them
to retire unmolested to Placentia on the Po,
while the Gauls withdrew to their own country.

The sequel is obscure, though some writers
say that Scipio, after he had joined forces with
his colleague, overran the country of the Boii
and Ligurians as far as the woods and marshes
allowed him to proceed. In any case he went
there, for it is stated that he returned from
Gaul to hold the elections. One other incident
of his term of office was that, on his proposal,
the Senators were for the first time allotted re-
served and separate seats at the Roman games.
While many held that this was an honour which
ought to have been accorded long before, others
opposed it vehemently, contending that " every
addition made to the grandeur of the Senate was
a diminution of the dignity of the people," that
it distilled class feeling, and if the ordinary seats
had been good enough for five hundred and
thirty-eight years, why should a change be made
now. " It is said that even Africanus himself
at last became sorry for having proposed that
matter in his consulship : so difficult is it to
bring people to approve of any alteration of
long-standing customs " (Livy).

All very petty ; and yet Scipio's good-natured

consideration for the comfort and dignity of others—it could not enhance his own—may have contributed to weaken his old influence with the people, who had been his support against the short-sighted Senators.

After the election of his successors, Scipio retired once more into private life, instead of taking a foreign province, as retiring consuls so often did. This circumstance has led one or two of the latter Roman historians to search for a motive. Thus Cornelius Nepos, the biographer of Cato, says that Scipio wanted to remove Cato from his province of Spain and become his successor, and that failing to obtain the Senate's assent, Scipio, to show his displeasure, retired into private life when his consulship was ended. Plutarch also, in his life of Cato, contradicts this, and says that Scipio actually succeeded Cato in Spain. Apart from the known historical inaccuracies of both these later writers, such pettiness would be inconsistent with all the assured facts of Scipio's character. We know that Cato and Scipio were always at variance, but the animosity, so far as speeches are recorded, was all on the side of Cato, to whom Scipio's Greek culture was as a red rag to a bull, and not less his moderation towards Carthage. The man whose parrot cry was *Delenda est Carthago*—fit ancestry of the Yellow Press—could not brook the man whose loftier soul and reputation stood in his way, nor his narrow spirit rest until he had brought about the destruction both of Carthage and Scipio. Their quarrel, if one-sided spite can be so called, dated from Zama, when Cato—serving as quæstor under Scipio, and already hating his Greek habits so much that he would not live in the same quarters—took violent exception to his general's lavish generosity to the soldiers in the distribution of the spoil.

Fortunately there are external facts which demolish the statements of both Nepos and Plutarch on this matter. A decision to disband Cato's army in Spain was made by the Senate at the same time as they refused Scipio's request to allot Macedonia as his consular province, and disbanded that army also. Cato accordingly returned, and received a triumph at the outset of Scipio's consulship. As there was no army there was obviously no post for a proconsul, which shows the futility of the statement that Scipio desired to go to Spain at the end of his consulship.

His real motive, however, in staying at Rome instead of seeking some other foreign province is not difficult to guess. He had predicted the danger from Antiochus, and as the Senate's refusal to anticipate it made a struggle inevitable, Scipio would wish to be on hand, ready for the call that he felt sure would come. He was right, for Hannibal was even then proposing to Antiochus an expedition against Italy, maintaining as ever that a campaign in Italy was the only key to Rome's defeat, because such invasion crippled the full output of Rome's man-power and resources. As a preliminary Hannibal proposed that he should be given a force to land in Africa and raise the Carthaginians, while Antiochus moved into Greece and stood by, ready for a spring across to Italy when the moment was ripe.

An envoy of Hannibal's, a Tyrian called Aristo, was denounced by the anti-Hannibalic party at Carthage. Aristo escaped, but the discovery caused such internal dissension that Masinissa thought the moment ripe to encroach on their territory.

The Carthaginians sent to Rome to complain, and he also to justify himself. The embassy of the former aroused uneasiness by their account of Aristo's mission and escape, and the envoys of Masinissa fanned this flame of suspicion. The Senate decided to send a commission to investigate, and Scipio was nominated one of the three, but after making an inquiry "left everything in suspense, their opinions inclining neither to one side or the other." This failure to give a verdict is hardly to the credit of Scipio, who had the knowledge and the influence with both

parties to have settled the controversy on the
spot. But Livy hints that the commissioners
may have been acting on instructions from the
Senate to abstain from a settlement, and adds
that in view of the general situation " it was
highly expedient to leave the dispute unde-
cided." By this he presumably means that as
Hannibal was meditating an invasion it was
policy to keep the Carthaginians too occupied to
support him.

At the end of the year an incident occurred
that sheds a significant light—rather twilight—
on Scipio's career. The two candidates for the
patrician vacancy as consul were Lucius Quinctius
Flamininus, brother of the victor of Cynoscephalæ, and Publius Cornelius Scipio, namesake
and half-brother to Africanus.

The upshot is aptly told by Livy : " Above
everything else, the brothers of the candidates,
the two most illustrious generals of the age,
increased the violence of the struggle. Scipio's
fame was the more splendid, and in proportion
to its greater splendour, the more obnoxious to
envy. That of Quinctius was the most recent,
as he had received a ' triumph ' that same year.
Besides, the former had now for almost two years
been continually in people's sight ; which circumstance, by the mere effect of satiety, causes
great characters to be less revered."   " All

Quinctius's claims to the favour of the public
were fresh and new; since his triumph, he had
neither asked nor received anything from the
people; ' he solicited votes,' he said, ' in favour
of his own brother, not of a half-brother; in
favour of his *legatus* and partner in the conduct
of the war ' "—his brother having commanded
the fleet against Philip of Macedon. " By these
arguments he carried his point." Lucius Quinctius was elected, and Scipio Africanus received
a further rebuff when Lælius, his old comrade
and lieutenant, failed to secure election as
plebeian consul despite Scipio's canvassing. The
crowd, eternally fickle and forgetful, preferred
the rising star to the setting sun.

Meantime the war clouds were gathering in the
East. Antiochus had safeguarded his rear by
marrying his daughter to Ptolemy, King of
Egypt. He then advanced to Ephesus, but lost
time by waging a local campaign with the Pisi-
dians. Across the Ægean, the Ætolians were
labouring hard to stir up war against the Romans,
and to find allies for Antiochus. Rome, on the
contrary, was weary and exhausted with years
of struggle, and sought by every means to postpone or avert a conflict with Antiochus. To
this end the Senate sent an embassy to him,
and Livy states that, according to the history
written in Greek by Acilius, Scipio Africanus was

employed on this mission. The envoys went to Ephesus, and while halting there on their way "took pains to procure frequent interviews with Hannibal, in order to sound his intentions, and to remove his fears of danger threatening him from the Romans." These meetings had the accidental and indirect but important consequence that the report of them made Antiochus suspicious of Hannibal.

But the main interest to us of these interviews, assuming that Acilius's witness is reliable, is the account of one of the conversations between Scipio and Hannibal. In it Scipio asked Hannibal, "Whom he thought the greatest captain?" The latter answered, "Alexander . . . because with a small force he defeated armies whose numbers were beyond reckoning, and because he had overrun the remotest regions, merely to visit which was a thing above human aspirations." Scipio then asked, "To whom he gave the second place?" and Hannibal replied, "To Pyrrhus, for he first taught the method of encamping, and besides no one ever showed such exquisite judgment in choosing his ground and disposing his posts; while he also possessed the art of conciliating mankind to himself to such a degree that the natives of Italy wished him, though a foreign prince, to hold the sovereignty among them, rather than the Roman people. . . ."

On Scipio proceeding to ask, " Whom he esteemed the third ? " Hannibal replied, " Myself, beyond doubt." On this Scipio laughed, and added, " What would you have said if you had conquered me ? " " Then I would have placed Hannibal not only before Alexander and Pyrrhus, but before all other commanders."

" This answer, turned with Punic dexterity, and conveying an unexpected kind of flattery, was highly grateful to Scipio, as it set him apart from the crowd of commanders, as one of incomparable eminence."

From Antiochus this embassy gained no direct result, for the " king of kings " was too swollen with pride on account of his Asiatic successes, too sure of his own strength, to profit by the examples of Carthage and Macedon. His standards of military measurement were strictly quantitative.

Realising at last that war was inevitable and imminent, the Roman Senate set about the preparations for this fresh struggle. As a first step they pre-dated the consular election so as to be ready for the coming year ; the new consuls were Publius Scipio, the rejected of the previous year, and Manius Acilius. Next, Bæbius was ordered to cross over with his army from Brundisium (Brindisi) into Epirus, and envoys were sent to all the allied cities to counteract Ætolian

propaganda. The Ætolians, nevertheless, gained
some success by a mixture of diplomacy and
force, and besides causing general commotion
throughout Greece, did their best to hasten the
arrival of Antiochus. Had his energy approxi-
mated to his confidence, he might well have
gained command of Greece before the Romans
were able to thwart him. Further, to his own
undoing, he abandoned Hannibal's plan and the
expedition to Africa, from a jealousy inspired
fear that if Hannibal were given an executive
rôle public opinion would regard him as the real
commander. Even when he made his belated
landing in Greece, with inadequate forces, he
missed such opportunity as was left by frittering
away his strength and time in petty attacks
against the Thessalian towns, and in idle pleasure
at Chalcis.

Meantime, at Rome the consuls cast lots for
their provinces ; Greece fell to Acilius, and the
expeditionary force which he was to take assembled at Brundisium. For its supply, com-
missaries had been sent to Carthage and Numidia
to purchase corn. It is a tribute alike to the
spirit in which the Carthaginians were seeking
to fulfil their treaty with Rome, and to Scipio's
wise policy after Zama, that they not only offered
the corn as a present, but offered to fit out a
fleet at their own expense, and to pay in a lump

sum the annual tribute money for many years
ahead. The Romans, however, whether from
proud self-reliance or dislike of being under an
obligation to Carthage, refused the fleet and the
money, and insisted on paying for the corn.

In face of all these preparations, Antiochus
awoke to his danger too late. His allies, the
Ætolians, provided only four thousand men, his
own troops delayed in Asia, and in addition he
had alienated Philip of Macedon, who stood
firm on the Roman side. With a force only ten
thousand strong he took up his position at the
pass of Thermopylæ, but failed to repeat the
heroic resistance of the immortal Spartans, and
was routed. Thereupon, forsaking his Ætolian
allies to their fate, Antiochus sailed back across
the Ægean.

Rome, however, was unwilling to rest content
with this decision. She realised that in Greece
her army had defeated only the advanced guard
and not the main body of Antiochus's armed
strength, and that unless he was subdued he would
be a perpetual menace. Further, so long as he
dominated Asia Minor from Ephesus, her loyal
allies, the Pergamenes and Rhodians, and the
Greek cities on the Asiatic side of the Ægean,
were at his mercy. All these motives impelled
Rome to counter-invasion.

Once more Hannibal's grand strategical vision

proved right, for he declared that "he rather
wondered the Romans were not already in Asia,
than had doubts of their coming." This time
Antiochus took heed of his great adviser, and
strengthened his garrisons as well as maintaining
a constant patrol of the coast.

CHAPTER XIV.

THE LAST LAP.

ROME, faced with a great emergency—second only to that of the Hannibalic War,—looked for its new saviour in its old. If the danger was less, and less close, the risk at least must have seemed greater, for her armies were venturing into the unknown. The first great trial of strength between Rome and Asiatic civilisation was about to be staged, and the theatre of war was alarmingly distant, connected with the homeland by long and insecure lines of communication. The spur of emergency quickens the memory, and Rome in her fresh hour of trial remembered the man who had saved her in the last, and who had been standing by for several years ready for the occasion which he had prophesied to deaf ears. Yet Scipio Africanus did not himself stand for the consulship—why it is difficult to guess. It may have been that he deemed the forces of jealousy too strong, and wanted to take no risks, or that affection and sympathy for his brother

Lucius, a defeated candidate the year before, inspired Africanus to give the latter his chance. Africanus had glory enough, and all through his career he had been ready to share his glory with his assistants. He left envy of others' fame to lesser men. His aim was service, and in any case he knew that if Lucius was consul, he himself would exercise the real power—Lucius was welcome to the nominal triumph.

His brother's election was secured, and with him, as plebeian consul, was elected Gaius Lælius, the old assistant of Africanus. It may be that Scipio worked for this, in order to ensure that to whichever Greece fell as a province he would be able to exercise an influence on the operations. As it happened, however, the double election put him in the unpleasant position of having to support his brother against his friend. For both consuls naturally desired Greece, which meant the command against Antiochus. Lælius, who had a powerful interest with the Senate, asked the Senate to decide—drawing lots was too uncertain for his taste. Lucius Scipio thereupon asked time to seek advice, and consulted Africanus, "who desired him to leave it unhesitatingly to the Senate." Then, when a prolonged debate was anticipated, Africanus arose in the Senate and said that "if they decreed that province to his brother, Lucius Scipio, he would

go along with him as his lieutenant." This
proposal " being received with almost universal
approbation," settled the dispute and was carried
by an almost unanimous vote.

Though it is clear that Africanus planned this
result, the fact does not lessen our appreciation
of the nobility of a man who, after being the
most illustrious commander in Rome's history,
would stoop to take a subordinate position.
If the means was diplomatic, the motive was
of the purest—to save his country, leaving to
another the reward.   Apart from blood ties, he
doubtless felt more sure of real control through
his brother than through Lælius—though Lucius's
obstinacy with the Ætolians refutes Mommsen's
verdict that he was " a man of straw."   Two
good leaders in the same command are not a
good combination.   It says much for both
Scipio Africanus and Lælius that this act did
not break down their friendship, and it is a
proof of the latter's generous nature, if also of
the former's transcendent qualities, that in later
years Lælius gave Polybius such testimony of
Scipio's greatness.

In addition to the two legions which he was to
take over in Greece from Acilius, the consul
was given three thousand Roman foot and one
hundred horse, and another five thousand foot
and two hundred horse from the Latin con-

federates. Further, directly it was known that Africanus was going, four thousand veterans of the Hannibalic War volunteered in order to serve again " under their beloved leader."

The expedition set forth in March (the Roman July), 190 B.C., but the advance into Asia was to be delayed because of the Senate's obstinacy in refusing to grant reasonable peace terms to the Ætolians, so driving them to take up arms anew and maintain a stubborn warfare in their mountain strongholds. It is curious that Scipio, who had always contributed to his military object by the moderation of his political demands, should now be blocked by others' immoderation.

When the Scipios landed in Epirus they found their destined army thoroughly embroiled by Acilius in this guerilla warfare. Africanus went ahead while his brother followed with his main body. On arrival at Amphissa, Athenian envoys met them, who, addressing first Africanus and afterwards the consul, pleaded for leniency to the Ætolians. " They received a milder answer from Africanus, who, wishing for an honourable pretext for finishing the Ætolian war, was directing his view towards Asia and King Antiochus." Apparently Africanus, with his habitual foresight, had actually inspired this mission of the Athenians, and another to the Ætolians. Scipio could have given points even to Colonel

House as an ambassador of peace as a means to victory. As a result of Athenian persuasion, the Ætolians sent a large embassy to the Roman camp, and from Africanus received a most encouraging reply. But when the decision was referred to the consul, as was necessary, his reply was uncompromising—he put his fist through the web his brother had so delicately woven. A second embassy met with the same obstinate refusal. Then the principal Athenian envoy advised the Ætolians to ask simply for a six months' armistice in order that they might send an embassy to Rome. The real source of this advice is too obvious to require any guess. Accordingly the Ætolian envoys came back, and "making their first application to Publius Scipio, obtained, through him, from the consul a suspension of arms for the time they desired."

Thus by diplomacy Africanus secured his lines of communication and released his army; the determination with which he sought a peaceful solution, and avoided being embroiled in a side-show, is an object-lesson in economy of force and the maintenance of the true objective.

The consul, having taken over the army from Acilius, decided to lead his troops into Africa through Macedonia and Thrace—taking the long land instead of the short sea route, because Antiochus had one fleet at Ephesus and another being raised by Hannibal in Phœnicia specially to prevent their crossing by sea. Africanus, while approving of this route, told his brother that everything depended on the attitude of Philip of Macedon; "for if he be faithful to our Government he will afford us a passage, and all provisions and material necessary for an army on a long march. But if he should fail you in this, you will find no safety in any part of Thrace. In my opinion, therefore, the King's dispositions ought to be ascertained first of all. He will best be tested if whoever is sent comes suddenly upon him, instead of by pre-arrangement."

Acting on this advice, as instinct with security as with psychology, Tiberius Gracchus, a specially active young man, was sent, riding by relays of horses, and so fast that he travelled from Amphissa to Pella—from the Gulf of Corinth almost to Salonika—in under three days, and caught Philip in the middle of a banquet—"far gone in his cups." This helped to remove suspicion that he was planning any counter-move, and next day Gracchus saw provision dumps prepared, bridges made over rivers, and hill roads buttressed—ready for the coming of the Roman army.

He then rode back to meet the army, which was thus able to move through Macedonia with

confidence. On their passage through his domains
Philip met and accompanied them, and Livy
relates that " much geniality and good humour
appeared in him, which recommended him much
to Africanus, a man who, as he was unparalleled
in other respects, was not averse to courteousness
unaccompanied by luxury." The army then
pushed on through Thrace to the Hellespont—
the Dardanelles,—taking the same route apparently as Xerxes, in an opposite direction.

Their crossing of the Dardanelles had been
smoothed for them as much by the mistakes
of Antiochus as by the action of their own fleet.
Livius, the Roman naval commander, had sailed
for the Dardanelles, in accordance with instructions, in order to seize the fortress which
guarded the passage of the Narrows. Sestos—
modern Maidos—was already occupied, and
Abydos—now Chanak—parleying for surrender,
when news reached Livius of the surprise and
defeat of the allied Rhodian fleet at Samos.
He abandoned his primary object—an action
which might have upset Scipio's plans—and
sailed south to restore the naval situation in
the Ægean. However, after some rather aimless
operations, the arrival of Hannibal's fleet and its
defeat—in his first and last sea battle—cleared
the situation in the Mediterranean. A second
victory in August, this time over Antiochus's

Ægean fleet, ensured for the Romans command of the sea.

With Antiochus, the loss of it led him into a move, intended for safety, that was actually the reverse. Despairing of being able to defend his possessions across the Dardanelles, he ordered the garrison to retire from Lysimachia, " lest it should there be cut off by the Romans." Now Lysimachia stood close to where Bulair stands to-day, and there is no need to emphasise how difficult it would have been to force those ancient Bulair Lines, commanding the isthmus of the Gallipoli peninsula. The garrison might well have held out till winter. Perhaps another factor, apart from the naval defeat, was his failure to gain the alliance of Prusias, King of Bithynia—a country whose sea coast lay partly on the Black Sea and partly on the Sea of Marmora. Antiochus sent to play on his fears of being swallowed by Rome, but once again Scipio's grand strategical vision had led him to foresee this move and take steps to checkmate it. Months before he reached Gallipoli, Scipio had written a letter to Prusias to dispel any such fears. " The petty chieftains in Spain," he wrote, " who had become allies, he had left kings. Masinissa he had not only re-established in his father's kingdom, but had put him in possession of that of Syphax "—a clever hint !

The double news of the naval victory and the
evacuation of Lysimachia reached the Scipios
on arrival at Ænos (Enos), and, considerably
relieved, they pressed forward and occupied
the city.   After a few days' halt, to allow the
baggage and sick to overtake them, they marched
down the Chersonese—the Gallipoli peninsula,—
arrived at the Narrows, and made an unopposed
crossing.   They crossed, however, without Africanus, who was detained behind by his religious
duties as one of the Salian priests.   The rules
of his order compelled him during this festival
of the Sacred Shields to remain wherever he was
until the month was out—and without Africanus
the army had lost its dynamo, so that "he
himself was a source of delay, until he overtook
the rest of the army."   Unnecessary delay was
far from one of his military characteristics, so
that the incident serves to suggest that his
piety was genuine and not merely a psychological
tool to inspire his troops.   While the army was
waiting for him, an envoy came to the camp
from Antiochus, and as he had been ordered
by the king to address Africanus first, he also
waited for him before discussing his mission !

"In him he had the greatest hope, besides
that his greatness of soul, and the fulness of his
glory, tended very much to make him inclined
to peace, and it was known to all nations what

sort of a conqueror he had been, both in Spain
and afterwards in Africa ; and also because his
son was then a prisoner with Antiochus " (Livy).
How the son was captured is uncertain, whether
in a distant cavalry reconnaissance, or earlier
at sea, as Appian suggests.

At a full council the Syrian envoy put forward
a basis for peace—that Antiochus would give
up the Greek cities in Asia Minor allied to Rome,
as he had already evacuated Europe, and would
pay the Romans half the expenses of the war.
The council regarded these concessions as inadequate, contending that Antiochus should
give up all the Greek seaboard on the Ægean,
and, in order to establish a wide and secure
neutral zone, relinquish possession of all Asia
Minor west of the Taurus mountains. Further,
he ought to pay all the expense of the war, as
he had caused and initiated it.

Thus rebuffed, the envoy sought a private interview with Africanus, according to his orders.
"First of all he told him that the King would
restore his son without a ransom ; and then,
as ignorant of the disposition of Scipio as he
was of Roman manners, he promised an immense
weight of gold, and, save for the title of king,
an absolute partnership in the sovereignty—if
through his means Antiochus should obtain
peace." To these advances Scipio replied, " I

am the less surprised that you are ignorant of
the Romans in general, and of me, to whom
you have been sent, when I see that you do not
realise the military situation of the person
from whom you come. You ought to have kept
Lysimachia to prevent our entering the Chersonese (Gallipoli), or to have opposed us at the
Hellespont to hinder our passing into Asia, if
you meant to ask peace as from people anxious
as to the issue of the war. But after leaving the
passage into Asia open, and receiving not only
a bridle but a yoke,[1] what negotiation on equal
terms is left to you, when you must submit to
orders ? I shall consider my son as a very great
gift from the generosity of the King. I pray to
the gods that my circumstances may never
require others ; my mind certainly never will
require any. For such an act of generosity to
me he shall find me grateful, if for a personal
favour he will accept a personal return of gratitude. In my public capacity, I will neither
accept from him nor give anything. All that
I can give at present is sincere advice. Go, then,
and desire him in my name to cease hostilities,
and to refuse no terms of peace " (Livy).
Polybius's version of the last sentence is a shade

---

[1] Polybius's version is, "having not only submitted to the
bridle, but allowed the rider to mount "—and while less graphic
it sounds more to the point, and more probable.

different : " In return for his promise in regard
to my son, I will give him a hint which is well
worth the favour he offers me—make any con-
cession, do anything, rather than fight with the
Romans."

This advice had no effect on Antiochus, and
he decided to push on his military preparations,
which were already well in hand. The consular
army then advanced south-east, by way of
Troy, towards Lydia. " They encamped near
the source of the Caicus river, preparing provisions for a rapid march against Antiochus, in
order to crush him before winter should prevent
operations." Antiochus faced them at Thyatira
—modern Akhissar. At this moment, just as
the curtain was about to rise on the final act,
and Scipio reap the reward of his strategy, fate
stepped in. He was laid low by sickness, and had
to be conveyed to Elæa on the coast. Hearing
of this, Antiochus sent an escort to take back
his son to him. This unexpected return of his
son was so great a relief to Scipio's mind as to
hasten his recovery from the illness. To the
escort he said, " Tell the King that I return him
thanks, that at present I can make him no other
return but my advice ; which is, not to come to
an engagement until he hears that I have rejoined
the army "—by this Scipio evidently meant that if
he was in charge Antiochus's life at least was safe.

Although the king had a vast army of sixty-two thousand foot and more than twelve thousand horse, he deemed this advice sufficiently sound to fall back behind the Hermus river, and there at Magnesia—modern Minissa—fortify a strong camp. The consul, however, followed him, and seeing that he refused battle called a council of war. Though the Romans only counted two legions, the equivalent of two allied legions, and some local detachments—about thirty thousand all told,—their verdict was unanimous. "The Romans never despised any enemy so much." However, they did not have to storm his camp, for on the third day, fearing the effect of inaction on the moral of his troops, Antiochus came out to offer battle.

Though the Roman victory was ultimately decisive, they clearly missed the tactical mastery of Africanus, and were even in trouble, if not in jeopardy, for a time. For while the Romans were driving in the enemy's centre, and the mass of their cavalry were attacking the enemy's left flank, Antiochus himself with his right wing cavalry crossed the river—left almost unguarded—and fell on the consul's left flank. The troops there were routed and fled to the camp, and only the resolution of the tribune left in charge rallied them and staved off the danger until reinforcements came. Foiled here and seeing a

heavy concentration developing against him,
Antiochus fled to Sardis, and the survivors of
his broken army followed. Further resistance
was hopeless, his western dominions crumbling
all around him, and the subject States making
their peace with Rome. He therefore retired to
Apamea, and from there sent a peace mission
to the Consul at Sardis, whither Africanus came
from Elæa as soon as he was fit to travel.

Before the mission arrived the terms had
been decided on, and it was agreed that Africanus
should deliver them. " Scipio began by saying
that victory never made the Romans more
severe than before." The conditions were the
same as had been offered before Magnesia,
when the issue was still open ; not a whit augmented because of Antiochus's present helplessness. Antiochus was to retire to the other side
of the Taurus range ; to pay fifteen thousand
Euboic talents towards the expenses of the war,
part at once and the rest in twelve annual instalments, and to hand over twenty selected
hostages as pledge of his good faith. In addition
Antiochus was to give up Hannibal, as it was
" clear that the Romans could never hope to
enjoy peace wherever he was," and certain
other notorious instigators of the war. Hannibal,
however, getting news of this clause, took refuge
in Crete.

The notable feature of these terms, as of those in Africa and Greece, was that the Romans sought security and prosperity merely. So long as Scipio guided Rome's policy, annexation, with all its dangers and troubles, is eschewed. His object is simply to ensure the peaceful predominance of Roman interests and influence, and to secure them against external dangers. It was true grand strategy which, instead of attempting any annexation of Antiochus's normal domains, simply compelled him to retire behind an ideal strategic boundary—the Taurus mountains, and built up a series of sovereign buffer States as a second line of defence between the Taurus range and the Ægean Sea. These were definitely the allies of Rome and not her subjects, and Asia Minor was organised for security by strengthening and rewarding the allies who had been faithful throughout the war. How might the course of history have been changed had not Scipio's successors reversed his policy and entered upon the fateful path of annexation ? When the barbarian invasions came they found the Mediterranean world composed of States so thoroughly Romanised that they had long since forgotten the feel of their fetters, yet from this one fact so atrophied as to be a drain and a weakness to Rome. Instead of the ring of virile outposts planned by Scipio, a ring of political eunuchs.

It is an amusing last comment on the settlement with Antiochus, and the removal of the last danger to Rome in the Mediterranean, that on Lucius Scipio's return to Rome " he chose to be called Asiaticus, that he might not be inferior to his brother in point of a surname." He also took steps to ensure that his " triumph " was more splendid in display than that of Africanus over Carthage. The only reward of Africanus was that for a third time he was nominated Prince of the Senate.

CHAPTER XV.

DUSK.

THE moderation and far-sighted policy of Scipio, which had undermined his influence in the years succeeding Zama, was now to cause his political ruin. The sequence of events is somewhat hazy, but their outline is clear. The narrow-minded party, led by Cato, who could not be content with the disarming of the enemy but demanded their destruction, were so chagrined at this fresh peace of mercy and wisdom that they vented their anger on its author. Unable to revoke the peace, they schemed to compass the downfall of Scipio, and fastened on the suggestion of bribery as the most plausible charge. Perhaps, quite honestly, men like Cato could conceive no other cause for generosity to a vanquished foe. However, they seem to have been clever enough not to assail the stronger brother first, but rather, aiming at weakness instead of strength, to strike at Africanus indirectly through his brother.

The first move seems to have been the prosecution of Lucius for misappropriation of the indemnity paid by Antiochus. Africanus was so indignant at the charge that, when his brother was in the act of producing his account books, he took them from him, tore them in pieces, and threw them on the floor of the Senate house. This action was unwise, but very human. Let any one put himself in the place of a man who by unparalleled services had rescued Rome from a deadly menace on her very hearth, and raised her to be the unchallenged and unchallengeable mistress of the world, and then, as he said indignantly, to be called on to account for four million sesterces when through him the treasury had been enriched by two hundred million. We must remember, too, that Scipio was a man suffering from an illness, soon to cause his death, and sick men are inclined to be irritable. Doubtless, too, that supreme self-confidence which marked him developed in later and sickness-ridden years into something approaching arrogance. Thus Polybius tells us that on one occasion, whether this or at the trial later, he bitingly retorted that, " It ill became the Roman people to listen to accusations against Publius Cornelius Scipio, to whom his accusers owed it that they had the power of speech at all." He had refused regal power when it had been thrust upon him, and been content to remain a private citizen, but he expected some measure of special consideration for his supreme services.

The defiant act, however, gave his enemies the opportunity they had longed for. Two tribunes, the Petilii, instigated by Cato, began a prosecution against him for taking a bribe from Antiochus in return for the moderation of his peace terms. The news set all Rome aflame with excitement and discussion. "Men construed this according to their different dispositions ; some did not blame the plebeian tribunes, but the public in general that could suffer such a process to be carried on " (Livy). A frequent remark was that " the two greatest States in the world proved, nearly at the same time, ungrateful to their chief commanders ; but Rome the more ungrateful of the two, because Carthage was subdued when she sent the vanquished Hannibal into exile, whereas Rome, when victorious, was for banishing the conqueror Africanus."

The opposing party argued that no citizen should stand so high as not to be answerable for his conduct, and that it was a salutary tonic that the most powerful should be brought to trial.

When the day appointed for the hearing came, " never was either any other person, or Scipio himself—when consul or censor,—escorted to the

Forum by a larger multitude than he was on
that day when he appeared to answer the charge
against him." The case opened, the plebeian
tribunes sought to offset their lack of any definite
evidence by raking up the old imputations about
his luxurious Greek habits when in winter quarters in Sicily and about the Locri episode. The
voices were those of the Petilii, but the words
were clearly Cato's. For Cato had not only
been the disciple of Fabius, but himself in Sicily
had made the unfounded allegations which the
commission of inquiry had refuted. Then after
this verbal smoke-cloud, they discharged the
poison gas. For want of evidence they pointed
to the restoration of his son without ransom, and
to the way Antiochus had addressed his peace
proposals to Scipio. "He had acted towards
the consul, in his province, as dictator, and not
as lieutenant. Nor had he gone thither with
any other view than it might appear to Greece
and Asia, as had long since been the settled
conviction of Spain, Gaul, Sicily, and Africa,
that he alone was the head and pillar of the
Roman power ; that a State which was mistress
of the world lay sheltered under the shade of
Scipio ; and that his nods were equivalent to
decrees of the Senate and orders of the people."

A cloud of words have rarely covered a poorer
case, their purpose, as Livy remarks, to "attack

by envy, as much as they can, him out of the reach of dishonour." The pleading having lasted until dusk, the trial was adjourned until next day.

Next morning when the tribunes took their seat and the accused was summoned to reply, the answer was characteristic of the man. No proof was possible either way, and besides being too proud to enter into explanations, he knew they would be wasted on his enemies as on his friends. Therefore, with the last psychological counter-stroke of his career, he achieves a dramatic triumph.

"Tribunes of the people, and you, Romans, on the anniversary of this day I fought a pitched battle in Africa against Hannibal and the Carthaginians, with good fortune and success. As, therefore, it is but decent that a stop be put for this day to litigation and wrangling, I am going straightway to the Capitol, there to return my acknowledgments to Jupiter the supremely great and good, to Juno, Minerva, and the other deities presiding over the Capitol and citadel, and will give them thanks for having, on this day, and at many other times, endowed me both with the will and ability to perform extraordinary services to the commonwealth. Such of you also, Romans, who choose, come with me and beseech the gods that you may have commanders like myself. Since from my seventeenth year until old age, you have always anticipated my years with honour, and I your honours with services."

Thereupon he went up towards the Capitol, and the whole assembly followed; at last, even the clerks and messengers, so that his accusers were left in a deserted forum. " This day was almost more famous owing to the favour of the Romans towards him, and their high estimation of his real greatness, than that on which he rode through Rome in triumph over Syphax and the Carthaginians." " It was, however, the last day that shone with lustre on Publius Scipio. For, as he could foresee nothing but the prosecutions of envy, and continual dispute with the tribunes, the trial being adjourned to a future day, he retired to his estate at Liternum, with a fixed determination not to attend the trial. His spirit was by nature too lofty, and habituated to such an elevated course of fortune, that he did not know how to act the part of an accused person, or stoop to the humble deportment of men pleading their cause " (Livy).

When the adjourned trial took place, and his name was called, Lucius Scipio put forward sickness as the cause for his brother's absence. The prosecuting tribunes refused to admit this, contending that it was merely his habitual disregard of the laws, and reproached the people for following him to the Capitol and for their lack of deter-

mination now : " We had resolution enough,
when he was at the head of an army and a fleet,
to send into Sicily . . . to bring him home, yet
we dare not now send to compel him, though a
private citizen, to come from his country seat to
stand his trial." They failed, however, to carry
their point. On Lucius appealing to the other
tribunes of the commons, the latter moved that,
as the excuse of sickness was pleaded, this should
be admitted, and the trial again adjourned.
One, however, Tiberius Gracchus, dissented, and
the assembly, knowing that there had been
friction between him and Scipio, expected a
more severe decision. Instead he declared that,
" Inasmuch as Lucius Scipio had pleaded sickness in excuse for his brother, that plea appeared
to him sufficient; that he would not suffer Publius
Scipio to be accused until he returned to Rome,
and even then, if Scipio appealed to him, he
would support him in refusing to stand his trial.
That Publius Scipio, by his great achievements,
by the honours received from the Roman people,
by the joint consent of gods and men, had risen
to such a height of dignity that, were he to stand
as a criminal under the rostrum and afford a
hearing to the insults of young men, it would
reflect more disgrace on the Romans than on
him."

Livy adds that Gracchus followed up his decree

by a speech of indignation : " Shall Scipio, the famous conqueror of Africa, stand at your feet —tribunes ? Was it for this he defeated and routed in Spain four of the most distinguished generals of Carthage and their four armies ? Was it for this he took Syphax prisoner, conquered Hannibal, made Carthage tributary to you, and removed Antiochus beyond the Taurus mountains—that he should crouch under two Petilii ? That you should gain the palm of victory over Publius Africanus ? " This speech, as well as his decree, made so strong an impression that the Senate called a special meeting and bestowed the warmest praise on Gracchus " for having consulted the public good in preference to private animosity." The prosecutors met with general hostility, and the prosecution was dropped.

" After that there was silence concerning Africanus. He passed the remainder of his life at Liternum, without a wish to revisit the city, and it is said that when he was dying he ordered his body to be buried there . . . that even his obsequies might not be performed in his ungrateful country."

That he died in voluntary exile at Liternum, probably in 183 B.C., seems assured, but his burial-place is less certain, and monuments of him existed both at Liternum and Rome. At the time of his death he was only fifty-two years

of age. By a fitting coincidence his great rival,
Hannibal, also died about the same time, and
probably in the same year—at the age of sixty-
seven. He had escaped, after Magnesia, to Crete,
and then taken refuge with Prusias of Bithynia.
The Roman Senate had the good sense to realise
that it was beneath their dignity to harry him
from his last refuge, but the local commander,
Flaminius, thought to gain distinction by in-
stigating Prusias to murder his trusting guest.
Hannibal thereupon defeated the assassins by
taking poison.

Even after Scipio's death, his enemies could
not rest. It rather " increased the courage of
his enemies, the chief of whom was Marcus
Porcius Cato, who even during his life was
accustomed to sneer at his splendid character."
Instigated by Cato, the demand was pressed for an
inquiry into the disposal of Antiochus's tribute.
Lucius was now the direct target, though his
brother's memory was still the indirect. Lucius
and several of his lieutenants and staff were
arraigned. Judgment was made against them,
and when Lucius declared that all the money
received by him was in the treasury, and therefore refused to give security for repayment, he
was ordered to prison. His cousin, Publius
Scipio Nasica, made a strong and convincing
protest, but the prætor declared that he had no

option, in view of the judgment, so long as
Lucius refused repayment. Gracchus again inter-
vened to save his personal enemies from disgrace.
Using his tribunitiary authority, he ordered
Lucius's discharge on account of his services to
Rome, and decreed instead that the prætor
should levy the sum due from Lucius's property.
The prætor thereupon sent to take possession of
it, "and not only did no trace appear of money
received from Antiochus, but the sum realised
by the sale of his property did not even equal
the amount of the fine " (Livy). This convincing
proof of the Scipios' innocence caused a revul-
sion of public feeling, " and the public hatred
which had been directed against the Scipios
recoiled on the prætor, his advisers, and the
accusers."

That his name should have been cleared after
death was, however, no consolation to the last
years of Africanus. " Ingratitude towards their
great men is the mark of strong peoples "—so the
proverb runs. Little wonder that Rome attained
the sovereignty of the ancient world.

CHAPTER XVI.

ROME'S ZENITH.

THERE is perhaps no military dictum so universally quoted as Napoleon's "Read and reread the campaigns of Alexander, Hannibal, Cæsar, Gustavus Adolphus, Turenne, Eugène, and Frederick ; take them for your model, that is the only way of becoming a great captain, to obtain the secrets of the art of war." In another of his maxims he said, "Knowledge of the great operations of war can only be acquired by experience and by the applied study of all the great captains. Gustavus, Turenne, and Frederick, as well as Alexander, Hannibal, and Cæsar, have all acted on the same principles."

Here Napoleon appears to single out a list of six, or possibly seven, commanders who stand out as supreme in the history of warfare. Whether consciously or unconsciously, there has been a general tendency among students of war to accept Napoleon's list as a standard classification of merit—not merely a haphazard mention—when

completed by the addition of his own name.
True, some have felt the absurdity of counting
Eugène as worthy to the exclusion of Marlborough, and others have dropped Turenne
because of a perhaps mistaken idea that greatness is synonymous with vastness of destruction,
or for the rather better reason that his record
lacked the decisive results gained by his com-
peers. In this way one finds that not a few
commentators have arrived at a list of three
ancient commanders—Alexander, Hannibal, and
Cæsar—and three modern—Gustavus, Frederick,
and Napoleon—as the Himalayan peaks of military history. That Frederick, with his gross
blunders and most unoriginal " oblique order,"
should receive preference over such consummate
artists as Turenne and Marlborough must remain
one of the mysteries of military criticism. This
is not the place to deal with the fallacy. Here
we are concerned with the great captains of
the ancient world, and so far as we desire
a comparison with the modern, Napoleon himself affords it, since his supremacy is hardly
questioned.

Let us therefore compare Scipio with these
three ancient great captains, by a threefold study
and test—as general, as man, and as statesman.
Any such comparison must be based on the conditions these men had to deal with, and on the

skill with which they turned these conditions to
their advantage.

Alexander, and to a hardly less degree Cæsar,
enjoyed the immense asset of having autocratic
power, complete control over the forces and resources available.   Even Hannibal, if poorly
supported, was immune from the petty interference with his operations against which Scipio,
like Marlborough later, had to contend.

Alexander's victories were won over Asiatic
hordes, whose lack of tactical order and method
offset their numerical superiority, and as Napoleon demonstrated in his well-known comment
on the Mamelukes, the defects of Asiatic troops
increased in ratio with their numbers.   No critic
places Clive in the first rank of great captains,
and but for the clear brilliance of his manœuvres
and the scale of his conquests Alexander would
suffer a like discount.   Cæsar, also, was hardly
more than an able " sepoy general " until Ilerda
and Pharsalus, and, as he himself is said to have
remarked, he went " to Spain to fight an army
without a general, and thence to the East to
fight a general without an army."   And even so,
Cæsar found himself, owing to an unwise dispersion of force, twice forced to fight under the
handicap of inferior strength.   In the first, at
Dyrrhacium, he suffered defeat, and though he
atoned for it at Pharsalus, this single first-class

victory is a slender base on which to build a
claim to supreme generalship.

But if we are to accept Napoleon's dictum
that "in war it is not men but the man who
counts," the most significant fact is that both
Alexander and Cæsar had their path smoothed
for them by the feebleness and ignorance of the
commanders who opposed them. Only Hannibal,
like Scipio, fought consistently against trained
generals, and even as between these the advantage of conditions is on Hannibal's side. For his
three decisive victories—the Trebia, Trasimene,
and Cannæ—were won over generals not only
headstrong and rash, but foolishly disdainful of
any tactics which savoured of craft rather than
of honest bludgeon work. Hannibal knew this
well—witness his remark to the troops who were
to lie concealed for the flank attack at the Trebia,
"You have an enemy blind to such arts of war."
Flaminius and Varro were mental Beefeaters,
and their names are instinctively bracketed in
history with those of Tallard, Daun, Beaulieu,
and MacMahon. Hannibal taught the Romans
the art, as distinct from the mechanism, of war,
and once they had profited by his instruction
his successes were limited. Marcellus and Nero
were capable of winning tricks off him, and if
they could not take a rubber neither could Hannibal. But in surveying Scipio's record, not

only do we find his tactical success unchequered, but that his opponents from the outset were generals trained in the Barcine school, and all the evidence goes to show that Hannibal's brothers, Hasdrubal and Mago, were no mean commanders. And the apex of Scipio's career, Zama, is unique in history as the only battle where one acknowledged great captain has, on his own, defeated another decisively.

Thus if conditions, and the extent to which they are not only met but turned to advantage, be the test, Scipio's pre-eminence is clear.

If the quality of a general's art be the test, universal opinion concedes that Hannibal excelled Alexander and Cæsar. Alexander's victories were rather triumphs of method, calculations working out with straightforward precision, but unmarked by any subtle variations and traps for the enemy. In Alexander, for all his greatness, still lingered traces of the Homeric hero, the glorification of the physical elements at the expense of the mental. It was this knight-errantry which led him to stake his life so often in the forefront of the battle, needlessly risking thereby the collapse of his plans and the lives of his army. To him might well be applied the rebuke made by Timotheus to Chares, when the former remarked: "How greatly ashamed I was at the siege of Samos when a bolt fell near

me ; I felt I was behaving more like an impetuous
youth than like a general in command of so
large a force." This mistaken Bayardism, too,
explains the absence of the subtler artistry in
his battles—it is epitomised in his rejection of
Parmenio's proposal to attack Darius by night
at Arbela, on the ground that he would not
" steal a victory." Cæsar's plans were assuredly
more difficult to guess, but he did not " mystify,
mislead, and surprise " to anything like the degree
that Hannibal attained. So general is the recognition of Hannibal's genius in this battle
art that he is commonly termed the supreme
tactician of history. Yet in ruse and strategem
the record of Scipio's battles is even richer.
Recall the unfortified front, the timing of the
direct assault, and the lagoon manœuvre at
Cartagena ; the double envelopment and reversal
of adverse ground conditions at Bæcula. The
change of hour and of dispositions, the refused
centre, the double oblique, and the double convergent flank blows at Ilipa. As Colonel Denison
notes in his ' History of Cavalry,' Ilipa is " generally considered to be the highest development
of tactical skill in the history of Roman arms."
I would suggest that the student of war, if he
considers it as a whole—from the mental opening
moves to the physical end of the pursuit,—cannot
but regard it as without a peer in all history.

Continuing, observe the use of ground first to
counter his enemy's numbers and then to force
him to fight separated battles, as well as the
wide turning movement, against Andobales.
Watch Scipio luring on his enemy into the
ambush at Salæca; study his masterpiece in
firing the Bagradas camps—the feint at Utica,
the sounding of the evening call, the timing of
and distinction between the two attacks, and the
subtlety with which he gains possession of the
main obstacle, the gates of the Carthaginian
camp, without a struggle. Note, later, his novel
use of his second and third lines as a mobile
reserve for envelopment at the Great Plains,
and the chameleon-like quickness with which
he translates his art into the naval realm when
he frustrates the attack on his fleet. Finally,
at Zama, where he is confronted with an opponent proof against the more obvious if more
brilliant stratagems, we see his transcendent
psychological and tactical judgment in his more
careful but subtly effective moves—the "lanes"
in his formation, and the synchronised trumpet
blast to counter the elephants; the deliberate
" calling off " of the *hastati*; the calculated
change of dispositions by which he overlaps
Hannibal's third, and main, line; the pause by
which he gains time for the return of his cavalry,
and their decisive blow in Hannibal's rear.

Is there such another collection of gems of
military art in all history ? Can even Hannibal
show such originality and variety of surprise ?
Moreover, if Hannibal's " collection " in open
battle is somewhat less full than Scipio's, in two
other essentials it is bare. Even his devoted
biographers admit that siegecraft, as with Frederick, was his weakness, and he has nothing to
set off against Scipio's storm of Cartagena,
which, weighed by its difficulties, its calculated
daring and skill, and its celerity, has no parallel
ancient or modern.

The other and more serious void in Hannibal's
record is his failure to complete and exploit his
victories by pursuit. Nowhere does he show a
strategic pursuit, and the lack of even a tactical
pursuit after the Trebia and Cannæ is almost
unaccountable. In contrast we have Scipio's
swift and relentless pursuit after Ilipa, and
hardly less after the battle on the Great Plains—
which alike for range and decisiveness are un-
approached until Napoleon, if then. In ancient
times Scipio has but one possible rival, Alexander,
and in his case there was repeatedly an in-
terregnum between the tactical and the strategic
pursuit, which caused a distinct debit against
his economy of force. For his turning aside
after Issus a strategic argument can be made
out, but for his delay after Granicus and Arbela

there appears no cogent reason save possibly
that of distance—the fact at least remains that
his campaigns offer no pursuit so sustained and
complete as that down the Bætis, or Guadalquiver. It may be suggested that Scipio did
not always pursue as after the two battles cited.
But an examination of his other battles show
that pursuit was usually either rash or unnecessary—rash after Bæcula, where he had two
fresh armies converging on him, and unnecessary
after Zama, where there was no enemy left to
be a danger.

From tactics we pass to strategy, and here a
preliminary demarcation and definition may sim-
plify the task of forming a judgment. Strategy
is too often considered to comprise merely military factors, to the overshadowing of the political
and economic, with which it is interwoven. The
fallacy has been responsible for incalculable
damage to the fabric of warring nations. When
such critics speak of strategy, they are thinking
almost solely of logistical strategy—the combination in time, space, and force of the military
pieces on the chessboard of war. Between logistical strategy and chess there is a distinct analogy.
But on a higher plane, and with a far wider
scope, is grand strategy, which has been defined
as " the transmission of power in all its forms in
order to maintain policy." " While strategy is

more particularly concerned with the movement
of armed masses, grand strategy, including these
movements, embraces the motive forces which
lie behind them, material and psychological.
. . . The grand strategist we see is, consequently,
also a politician and a diplomatist." [1]

As a logistical strategist Napoleon is unrivalled
in history—save possibly by the Mongol, Subutai,
from what we can piece together of the scanty
records of his campaigns. The ancients suffer,
in common with the modern precursors of Napoleon, the handicap that the organisation of armies
in their day did not permit of the manifold combinations that he effected, a handicap which
persisted until the divisional system was born
in the late eighteenth century, beginning with
De Broglie. Previously we find detachments, or
occasionally, as in Nero's classic move to the
Metaurus against Hasdrubal, a two-army combination, but the scope and variation of such
combination were inevitably narrow until armies
came to be organised in self-contained and independent strategic parts—the modern division or
army corps—just in time for the genius of Napoleon to exploit these new possibilities. But
within the inherent limitations of pre-Napoleonic
times, Scipio develops a range of strategical moves
which, it may be fairly claimed, is unequalled

[1] 'Reformation of War,' by J. F. C. Fuller.

in the ancient world. The hawk-like swoop on Cartagena, so calculated that none of the three Carthaginian armies could succour their base in time. The hardly less bold and calculated blow at Hasdrubal Barca before either Hasdrubal Gisco or Mago could effect a junction—how closely the margin of time worked out we know from Polybius. Nor is there any doubt whether these strategic moves were deliberate, as in many ascribed to ancient commanders on supposition by military critics who view old theatres of war through modern spectacles. Polybius and Livy both tell us that these calculations were in Scipio's mind. Again, the way in which Scipio stood guard over Hasdrubal Gisco while his detachment under Silanus moved and fell on Hanno and Mago before they had word of his approach. Swift as the march, as thorough was the defeat.

Next, the master move leading to Ilipa, whereby his direction of advance cut Hasdrubal and Mago off from their line of communication with Gades, which in the event of their defeat meant that retreat to their fortified base was barred by the river Bætis (Guadalquiver). The upshot showed both the truth of his calculation and the proof of the fact—the result was the annihilation of the Carthaginian armies. This seems the first clear example in history of a blow against the strategic flank. Here is born

the truth which Napoleon was to crystallise in
his cardinal maxim that " the important secret
of war is to make oneself master of the communications." Its initiation is sometimes claimed
for Issus, but at best Alexander's manœuvre was
on the battlefield, not in strategic approach,
while the simple explanation is that the sea prevented a move on the other flank and that the
bend in the river Pinarus dictated the direction
of it.

Admittedly Scipio's strategic intention at Ilipa
is a hypothesis, and not definitely stated in
Livy or Polybius; but the established facts of
the advance, and still more of its sequel, form a
chain of indirect evidence that could not be
firmer. Even Dodge, one of Scipio's consistent
detractors, emphasises this threat to the strategic
flank.

Before passing on to his African campaigns,
we may note Scipio's anticipation of, and trap
for Hannibal at Locri. Then note how, on landing in Africa, his first care is to gain a secure
base of operations, fulfilling the principle of
security before he passes to the offensive. See
him baulk the enemy's superior concentration
of strength by the " Torres Vedras " lines near
Utica. Note the rapidity with which he strikes
at Hasdrubal and Syphax at the Great Plain,
before their new levies can be organised and

consolidated, and how in the sequel he once more stands guard, this time over Carthage, while his detachment under Lælius and Masinissa knocks Syphax out of the war. Finally, there is his move up the Bagradas Valley by which he simultaneously compels Hannibal to follow, and facilitates his own junction with Masinissa's reinforcement from Numidia. So complete is his mastery on the strategical chessboard that he even selects the battlefield most favourable to the qualities of his own tactical instrument Then, Zama decided, he pounces on Carthage before the citizens can rally from the moral shock.

What, if any, mistakes can be set down on the debit side of his strategy? A study of military commentaries shows that his critics advance but three—that Hasdrubal Barca and Mago in turn escaped from Spain, and that Scipio did not lay siege to Carthage immediately on landing in Africa. The obvious reply is to ask how many times did Darius, a far more vital personal factor, escape Alexander, why Cæsar let slip Pompey after Pharsalus, or Hannibal fail to move on Rome after Trasimene or Cannæ— there were far less adequate reasons. But apart from the extreme difficulty of catching an individual without an army, it is hoped that the earlier chapters may have disposed of these empty criticisms. Even after Bæcula, Scipio

was still markedly inferior in strength to the
Carthaginian forces in Spain, and further, Hasdrubal was only able to elude Scipio's watch
and cross the Pyrenees with so weak a con-
tingent that he was forced to recruit in Gaul
for two years before he could advance on Italy.
Mago's escape was still more an individualistic
effort. As for the question of an immediate
advance on Carthage, Scipio would have been
an impetuous fool, not a general, if he had laid
siege to so vast a fortified city as Carthage with
the small original force that he carried into
Africa. The clearest proof of his wisdom in first
seeking a secure base of operations lies in the
overwhelming enemy concentration from which
he only escaped by his foresight in forming his
" Torres Vedras " lines.

In Alexander's record even his modern biographers do not suggest any notable examples
of logistical strategy, apart from certain swift
marches such as that from Pelium on Thebes.
There are no combinations or checks to enemy
combination. His strength lies in his grand
strategy, of which we shall speak later.

With Hannibal, too, his logistical strategy is
mainly a matter of direct marches and of admirable care to secure his communications, apart
from the very disputable purpose of his move
on the line of the Po which, in effect, separated

the elder Scipio from Sempronius, his fellow-consul; and secondly, his feint at Rome in the attempt to relieve the pressure on his allies at Capua, which, though clearly intended, was abortive. Against these must be set, first, the fact that the advantage of his hazardous march over the Alps was foiled of its purpose by the elder Scipio's quicker return from the Rhone by the Riviera route; second, the fact that he failed to prevent the junction of Sempronius with Scipio on the Trebia. Later, there are, among other indisputable failures, the neglect to exploit Cannæ even by the seizure of Canusium, let alone a thrust at Rome; the times his moves were parried by Fabius and Marcellus; Nero's brilliant deception by which Hannibal remained stationary and in the dark, while his brother was being crushed on the Metaurus. Finally, we see him outmanœuvred by Scipio in the preliminary moves before Zama. Outstandingly great as a tactician, Hannibal is not impressive as a strategist; less so, indeed, than several of Scipio's forerunners among the Roman generals.

Cæsar, in contrast, stands out more in logistical strategy than in tactics. But classic as are many of his moves in Gaul one has to remember that they were made against barbarians, not trained generals such as those with whom Scipio, Hannibal, Nero, and Marcellus had to contend.

Against Pompey's lieutenants in Spain he extricated himself with surpassing skill from a
critical position, into which perhaps he should
not have got. Then in Greece he threw away
his superiority of force by dispersion, and suffered
a severe defeat at Dyrrhacium, nearly disastrous
as he confessed when he said : " To-day the
victory had been the enemy's, had there been
any one among them to gain it." His retreat
was a masterly feat, if we overlook the quality
of his opponents, but later he failed in his attempt
to prevent the junction of Pompey and Scipio
Nasica, and had to fight at Pharsalus without
his detachments against a concentrated force.
That his tactics turned the balance does not
affect the reflection on his strategy.

If Scipio, then, may be given the palm for
logistical strategy among the ancients, how does
he compare with Napoleon ? We could adopt the
historical argument that a man must be judged
by the conditions and tools of his time, pointing
out not only the indivisible organisation with
which Scipio had to work, but that he was a
pioneer where Napoleon had the experience of
ages to build on. But we prefer rather to abandon
this sound and normal test, which inevitably
negatives true comparison, and admit frankly
Napoleon's supremacy in this sphere. The scales
are amply balanced by Scipio's superiority as

a tactician. By wellnigh universal opinion Napoleon's tactics were below his strategical level, and it is this compensating factor which has led military criticism to bracket Hannibal with Napoleon among the great captains—a factor which we suggest applies still more in Scipio's favour compared with Napoleon.

From logistical strategy we come to grand strategy. This lies in the domain of peace as much as in war, and hence for simplicity it may be well to deal with the grand strategy which contributed to the winning of wars, and reserve for our study of Scipio as statesman that part of his grand strategy which had its goal in the subsequent peace.

If our examination of the years 210-190 B.C. has achieved its historical purpose, it should be clear that Scipio showed an understanding of war in its three spheres—mental, moral, and physical, and of their interplay, such as is just dawning on the most progressive politico-military thought of to-day. Further, he translated this understanding into effective action in a way that we may possibly achieve in the next great war— more probably, we shall be fortunate to get out of the physical rut by 2000 A.D.

For proof of this claim look at the progressive and co-ordinated steps by which, starting from the valley in Rome's darkest hour, he climbs

steadily and surely upwards to the summit of
his aims, and plants Rome's flag on the sunlit
peaks of earthly power. Scipio is a mountaineer,
not a mere athlete of war. The vision that
selects his line of approach, and the diplomatic
gifts which enable him to surmount obstacles,
are for him what rock-craft is to a climber. His
realisation of the importance of securing his base
for each fresh advance is his snow-craft, and his
employment of military force his ice-axe.

Watch him, on arrival in Spain, make wide
inquiries about the position of the Carthaginian
forces, and the importance and topography of
Cartagena. His genius tells him that here is
the base and pivot of the Carthaginian power in
Spain, and shows him the feasibility, the way,
and the effect of such a stroke—at the moral
and economic rather than the purely military
objective.

Cartagena gained, note the wisdom which by
conciliating the citizens secures his acquisition
against internal treachery, and further enables
him to economise the garrison by converting the
citizens into active partners in the defence.
What a diplomatic coup is the prompt release
and care of the Spanish hostages. If Napoleon's
presence was worth an army corps, Scipio's
diplomacy was literally worth two. It converted
allies of the enemy into allies of his own.

There was grand strategy, too, in his wise
restraint from a further advance, in order to
allow the moral and political effect of Cartagena
and its sequel to develop. Thus Hasdrubal
Barca, seeing the Spanish sand trickling fast
from his end of the hour-glass to Scipio's, was
drawn into the offensive move which enabled
Scipio to beat him before the other Carthaginian
armies came up. Once more victory paves the
way for diplomacy, as that in turn will pave the
way for further victories. He sends home the
Spanish captives without ransom, and, still more
shrewdly, returns Masinissa's nephew loaded with
presents—surely never in history has the money
invested in presents brought a greater ultimate
dividend.

Next, note the rapidity with which Scipio nips
in the bud the incipient threat from Hanno, and
in contrast the constraint by which he avoids
wasting his force on a number of petty sieges
which could bring no commensurate profit. The
wider effect of Scipio's action in Spain also deserves notice, for Livy tells us that this year
Hannibal in Italy was for the first time reduced
to inaction, because he received no supplies from
home owing to Carthage being more anxious
about the retention of Spain.

Scipio's grand strategy was from now onwards
to lift the pressure off Rome in ever-increasing

degree. His success in Spain compelled the Carthaginians to invest there the forces that might have been decisive in Italy, and at Ilipa he wipes them off the military balance-sheet.

The instant that victory in Spain is sure, and before turning to the mere clearing operations, his grand strategical eye focusses itself on Africa. His daring visit to Syphax, his meeting with and despatch of Masinissa to Numidia—here are two strings to a bow which shall soon loose a shaft at the heart of Carthage. For an object-lesson in the selection of the true objective, and its unswerving maintenance in face of all obstacles and perils, the next few years are a beacon light for all time. He schemes, he prepares, he works unceasingly towards the goal. The military interference of the enemy is almost the least of his difficulties. Sexual passion frustrates one of his shrewdest diplomatic moves, but his plan is too flexible, too well conceived, for even this blow to have more than a transient effect. Jealous rivals, short-sighted politicians, military " diehards " do their best, or worst, to block his plan, and failing in this, to obstruct him and curtail his strength. He builds and trains a fresh army out of adventurers and disgraced troops. Yet he never makes a rash or a false move, mindful always of the principle of security. By diplomacy again he creates in Sicily a sure source of supply.

He sends a reconnoitring expedition to clear up
the African situation, and appreciating Masinissa's material weakness, refuses to be rushed
into a move before his own weapon is forged.
When he lands, his first efforts are directed to
gain a secure base of operations. And gauging
exactly the strength and weakness of Carthage
and of his own position, he adapts consummately
his immediate end to his existing means. Each
successive move is so directed as to subtract
from the military and political credit of Carthage
and transfer the balance to his own account. His
restraint when this ultimate goal is so close in
mileage, though not in reality, is almost miracu-
lous in a commander so youthful and so early
successful. But he has long realised that Syphax
and Masinissa are the two props of the Carthaginian power in Africa, and before he attempts
to turn this power out of its seat his first aim is
to upset its stability, by taking away one prop
and knocking away the other. Just as he has
gained this end, passion once more intervenes
to threaten his military achievement as it
previously thwarted his diplomacy, but the
psychological master-move by which he foils
Sophonisba's wiles averts the danger.

Now assured of security he aims at Carthage
itself, and characteristically pauses in sight of
Carthage to achieve, if possible, the supreme

economy of force of a moral victory instead of
the drain of a physical siege. The move succeeds,
and Carthage capitulates with Hannibal still
across the seas, helpless to aid. And when by
a gross breach of faith the treaty is violated,
Scipio is not caught off his guard. By a fresh
and rapid series of moves, a perfect combination
of military, economic, and psychological pieces,
he achieves the checkmate in a brief span of
time. Is there anything in history which for
continuity of policy, combination of forces—
material and moral,—and completeness of attainment can compare with it ? Scipio is the embodiment of grand strategy, as his campaigns
are the supreme example in history of its meaning.

Alexander certainly preceded Scipio as the
first grand strategist, but without arguing the
question how far his moral and economic action
was fortuitous rather than marked by the exquisite calculation of Scipio's, his task was much
simpler, and as a despot he had none of Scipio's
internal obstacles to surmount. It is, above all,
because of the close parallel with modern conditions, political and organic, that Scipio's grand
strategy is so living a study for us to-day.

Alexander's achievements may have excelled
Scipio's in scale—not really so much, for if
Alexander established for himself an empire
from the Danube to the Indus, which collapsed

on his death, Scipio built for Rome an empire
which stretched from the Atlantic to the Black
Sea and the Taurus mountains—an empire which
endured and increased. And whereas Alexander
built on the foundations laid by Philip, Scipio
came on the scene at a moment when the very
foundations of Roman power in Italy were shaken
by a foreign foe. There are grave blemishes,
too, on Alexander's strategy—while he was con-
solidating his offensive base in Asia Minor,
he was in acute danger of losing his home base
in Europe. By the disbandment of his fleet he
exposed the European coasts to the superior
Persian fleet, and Darius's one able commander,
Memnon, seized the chance to raise Greece,
where the embers of discontent smouldered in
Alexander's rear. Only Memnon's death saved
Alexander from disaster, and gained time for
him to carry out his plan of crippling Persian
sea power by land attack on their naval bases.
Again, by lack of strategical reconnaissance,
Alexander blundered past the army of Darius,
lying in wait in northern Syria, which moved
down and cut his communications, a danger
from which he only saved himself, facing about,
by tactical victory at Issus. It is well to contrast
this with Scipio's thorough strategical reconnaissance and search for information before
every move. If Alexander's grand strategy has

a narrow advantage by the test of quantity, Scipio's is clearly superior in quality.

In the comparison of Scipio with Napoleon, if the latter's superiority in logistical strategy is recognised, we have to set against this both his tactical and his grand strategical inferiority. As a grand strategist Napoleon's claims are marred not only by his failure to realise the aim of grand strategy—a prosperous and secure peace,—but by his several blunders over the psychology of his opponents, over the political and economic effects of his actions, and in the extravagant later use of his forces and resources.

Finally, let us point out that while Alexander had the military foundations laid by Philip to build on, while Hannibal built on Hamilcar, Cæsar on Marius, Napoleon on Carnot—Scipio had to rebuild on disaster.

From the comparison of generalship we pass to the comparison of character. Here, to enumerate at length the qualities which distinguished Scipio as a man would be wearisome. His moderation, his self-control, his human sympathy, his charm of manner, his magnetic influence over troops—shared by all the greatest captains,—his exaltation of spirit, these have shone through his deeds and speeches. Of his private life we know little save by inference. He married Æmilia, daughter of the consul

Æmilius Paullus who fell at Cannæ, the marriage
apparently taking place after his return from
Spain and before his departure for Africa.

From the solitary anecdote or two which
survive, the marriage seems to have been a
happy one, and Scipio to have shown more
deference to his wife's opinion than was common
at the time. That she had tastes too expensive
for Cato's liking seems assured; she was probably one of those leaders of Roman female
society against whom he directed his complaints—
that by wearing " a garment of various colours,
or riding in a carriage drawn by horses " in the
towns, they would undermine the social fabric
and create discontent. The indulgence shown
by Scipio to his wife, and his breach with tradition in treating her better than his slave, was
certainly one of the factors which rankled in
Cato's mind. Of the moral influence distilled in
the Scipio family life, the best proof is an indirect one. Their daughter Cornelia was given
in marriage to Tiberius Gracchus, apparently
after he had so generously defended Scipio's
reputation, and was the mother of the Gracchi.
The way in which she carried out their education,
and the principles with which she inspired these
future reformers, make one of history's noblest
pages.

Outside the domestic sphere, Scipio's influence

on social history rests on his love for and introduction of Greek literature and philosophy. " A man of great intellectual culture," he could speak and write Greek as well as he could Latin— he is said to have written his own memoirs in Greek. To his Greek studies he clearly owed that philosophy of life which permeates all his recorded acts and sayings. He seems to have taken the best elements from Greece and Rome, and to have blended them—refining the crudeness and narrowness of early republican Rome without diminishing its virility. So marked was his influence that he may, with some justice, be termed the founder of Roman *civilisation*. " To him is attributed the rise of manners, the origin of their taste for propriety, and of their love of letters." A rather touching instance of his own love of letters is enshrined in his friendship and admiration for the poet Ennius, a regard so profound that he left orders that after his death a bust of the poet should be placed with his in the tomb of the Scipios. Yet it was this very influence as an apostle of civilisation and of the humanities that earned him the bitter animosity, as it stimulated the fear, of Romans of the old school. Cato and his kind might have forgiven his military success and his self-confidence, but nothing but his downfall could atone for his crime in introducing Greek customs, philosophy, and literature. It is not unlikely that this damaged him, and undermined his influence even more than his contempt for pettier minds and his moderation to conquered foes. These are the only charges which his enemies could bring against his character, and in this fact lies perhaps the strongest proof of his superior moral nobility. For the malice of an enemy will fasten on any conceivable weakness, and thus the charges levied against a great man form a standard of moral measure which is one of the best of comparisons.

From this test Scipio alone of the great captains of antiquity emerges scatheless of any charge that suggests a definite moral blemish. It is true that we can discount most of the charges brought against Hannibal—impiety, avarice, perfidy, and cruelty beyond the customs of his day. But Alexander, whatever allowance we make in other accusations, stands convicted of want of self-control, violent outbursts of temper and prejudice, cruel injustice as to Parmenio, ambitious egotism verging on megalomania, and ruffianism in his cups. Alexander was tarred with the brush of Achilles.

Similarly, Cæsar's many great qualities cannot disguise his sexual license, his political corruption and intrigue, and the predominantly selfish motives which inspired his work and achieve-

ments. There are interesting parallels between
the careers of Cæsar and Scipio. Compare
Cæsar gaining the province of Gaul by intrigue
and threat, Scipio the province of Spain at the
call of his country in the hour of adversity.
Compare Cæsar forming and training an army
for the conquest of Rome, Scipio for the sal-
vation of Rome from her foreign foes. Compare
Cæsar crossing the Rubicon, Scipio the Bagradas
—and their objects. Compare Cæsar receiving
the honour of a triumph over fellow-Romans,
Scipio over Syphax and Hannibal. Lastly, if
it be true that " a man can be known by the
friends he keeps," compare Catiline with Lælius
and Ennius. Napoleon's saying that " Laurels
are no longer so when covered with the blood of
citizens," comes curiously from his lips. For
Napoleon's ambition drained the blood of France
as surely as Cæsar's spilt the blood of Rome.
It would suffice to strip the laurels from the brows
of both, and enhance the contrast with Scipio,
the supreme economist of blood and of force
in the selfless service of his country. It is not
difficult to guess why Napoleon should ignore
Scipio in his list of military models !

By any moral test Scipio is unique among the
greater captains, possessing a greatness and
purity of soul which we might anticipate, not
necessarily find, among the leaders of philosophy

or religion, but hardly among the world's supreme men of action. The clergyman who, a century ago, was Scipio's one English biographer, and whose work suffers by its brevity, its historical slips and the omission of all study of Scipio as a soldier, had yet one flash of rare insight and epigrammatic genius when he said that Scipio was " greater than the greatest of bad men, and better than the reputed best of good ones."

Last of all we turn to Scipio as statesman— that part of his grand strategy which lies definitely in the state of peace. The Abbé Seran de la Tour, who compiled a life of Scipio in 1739, dedicated it to Louis XV., and in his dedication wrote : " A king has only to take for his model the greatest man by far in the whole of Roman history, Scipio Africanus. Heaven itself seems to have formed this particular hero to mark out to the rulers of this world the art of governing with justice." The lesson, we are afraid, was lost on Louis XV., a man who at the council table " opened his mouth, said little, and thought not at all," whose life is as full of vulgar vice as it is bare of higher aims. We suspect the Abbé of a capacity for subtle sarcasm.

When Scipio came on the stage of history, Rome's power did not even extend over the whole of Italy and Sicily, and this narrow territorial sway was gravely menaced by the encroachments, and still more the presence, of Hannibal. At Scipio's death Rome was the unchallenged mistress of the whole Mediterranean world, without a single possible rival on the horizon. This period saw by far the greatest expansion in the whole of Roman history, and it was due either directly to Scipio's action, or made possible by him. But if territorially he stands out as the founder of the Roman Empire, politically his aim was not the absorption but the control of other Mediterranean races. He followed, but enlarged, the old Roman policy, his purpose not to establish a centralised, a despotic empire, but a confederation with a head, in which Rome should have the political and commercial supremacy, and over which her will should be paramount. Here lies the close parallel with modern conditions, which gives to the study of his policy a peculiar and vital interest. Cæsar's work paved the way for the decline and fall of Roman power. Scipio's work made possible a world community of virile States, acknowledging the overlordship of Rome, but retaining the independent internal organs necessary for the nourishment and continued life of the body politic. Had his successors possessed but a tithe of the wisdom and vision of Scipio, the Roman Empire might have taken a course analogous to that of the modern

British Empire, and by the creation of a ring of semi - independent and healthy buffer States around the heart of Roman power, the barbarian invasions might have been thwarted, the course of history changed, and the progress of civilisation have escaped a thousand years of coma and nearly as much of convalescence.

His peace terms alone would place Scipio on a pinnacle among the world's great conquerors— his entire absence of vindictiveness, his masterly insurance of military security with a minimum of hardship to the conquered, his strict avoidance of annexation of any civilised State. They left no festering sores of revenge or injury, and so prepared the way for the conversion of enemies into real allies, effective props of the Roman power. In the meaning of Scipio's name—a " staff "—was epitomised his grand strategy in war and peace.

The character of his policy was in tune with his character as a man, disdaining the tinsel glory of annexation as of kingship, for the solid gold of beneficent leadership. Scipio laboured for the good and greatness of Rome, but he was no narrow patriot, instead a true world states-man. The distinction between Scipio and Cæsar has been crystallised in the phrase, " Zama gave the world to Rome, Pharsalus gave it to Cæsar," but even this does not render Scipio full justice,

for he could look beyond the greatness of Rome's
glory to the greatness of her services to humanity.
Not an internationalist, he was a supra-nationalist
in the widest and best sense.

Attila was called the " scourge of the world,"
and with a difference only in degree most of the
great captains, from Hannibal to Napoleon,
have had no higher objective conception than
to thrash their enemies, or at best their country's
enemies, into submission.   Thus   this   fallacy
paved the way for a reaction equally short-
sighted, which led Green, in his ' History of the
English People,' to write :   " It is a reproach
of historians that they have turned history into
a mere history of the butchery of men by their
fellow-men," and to follow this up by the absurd
declaration that " war plays a small part in the
real story of European nations."   So arose a
very large modern school of historians who
sought, irrationally, to write history without
mentioning, let alone studying, war.   To ignore
the influence of war as a world-force is to divorce
history from science, and to turn it into a fairy
tale.   The grand strategy of Scipio is a signpost
pointing the true path of historical study.   Scipio
could administer military beatings at least as
effectively and brilliantly as any other of the
greater captains, but he saw beyond the beating
to its object.   His genius revealed to him that

peace and war are the two wheels on which the world runs, and he supplied a pole or axle which should link and control the two to ensure an onward and co-ordinated progress. Scipio's claim to eternal fame is that he was the staff, not the whip, of Rome and of the world.

281

BIBLIOGRAPHY.

AFTER due reflection and discussion with others, I have decided not to litter the actual pages of the book with footnote references, but to list the various historical sources in this bibliographical appendix. The modern fashion tends to treat an historical study as a literary card-index rather than as a book to be read, and in many instances this tendency is carried so far that the footnotes swamp the text. Experience suggests that even the barest footnote reference is a distraction to the reader's eye, and momentarily dams the flow of the narrative through his mind. For this reason I have omitted references from the actual pages except where they could be woven into the text, and if some readers hold that I err in this decision, I can at least plead that I do so in good company.

The ancient sources—all of which, except Polybius, require to be treated with critical caution—have been :—

Polybius, X. 2-20, 34-40 ; XI. 20-33 ; XIV. 1-10 ;
    XV. 1-19 ; XVI. 23 ; XXI. 4-25 ; XXIII. 14.
Livy, XXI.-XXII., XXV.-XXXIX.
Appian, *Punica, Hisp., Hann., Syr.*
Aulus Gellius, IV. 18.
Cornelius Nepos, XXXI.-XXXII. ; *Cato; Hannibal.*
Plutarch, *Cato; Æmilius Paullus; Tib. Gracchus.*
Valerius Maximus, III. 7.